NOT ONE MORE!

NEW DIRECTIONS IN RHETORIC AND MATERIALITY
Barbara A. Biesecker, Wendy S. Hesford, and Christa Teston, Series Editors

NOT ONE MORE!

FEMINICIDIO
ON THE BORDER

NINA MARIA LOZANO

THE OHIO STATE UNIVERSITY PRESS

COLUMBUS

Library of Congress Cataloging-in-Publication Control Number: 2018042720

Cover design by Susan Zucker
Text design by Juliet Williams
Type set in Adobe Minion Pro

♾ The paper used in this publication meets the minimum requirements of the American National Standard for Information Sciences—Permanence of Paper for Printed Library Materials. ANSI Z39.48-1992.

Written for the Mothers and family members of the disap-
peared and murdered women and girls in Ciudad Juárez. For
the activists who, in solidarity, continue to struggle for justice.
For the murdered and disappeared women and girls of Ciudad
Juárez. Your stories, histories, and lives will not be forgotten.

¡Ni Una Más!

!Ni Una Menos!

I dream of my daughter every night. And I always hug her. Always. I hug her and don't have the heart to tell her what they did to her. Until the last day, until my last breath, I will continue to look for her. I love her with all my heart, and will always. My daughter is with me; they haven't taken her from me. The fact that she's not physically here, doesn't mean she really isn't. It's what's kept me alive. I keep waiting for her. I keep looking for her. Even if they told me what they did to her. It means nothing.

—Susana, Mother of Maria Guadalupe Pérez Montes

CONTENTS

List of Illustrations   ix

Acknowledgments   xi

Preface   *Feminicidio in Ciudad Juárez*   xv

INTRODUCTION   New Materialism and Border Materialism   1

CHAPTER 1   Waves of Feminicidio   19

CHAPTER 2   Feminicidio and the "Enchanted" Assemblages of
                            Things   46

CHAPTER 3   Feminicidio, Public Memory, and "Thing Power"   69

CHAPTER 4   Feminicidio, Objects, and Affect   87

CHAPTER 5   Lifeless or "Vibrant Matter"?   107

CONCLUSION   123

Bibliography   137

Index   153

ILLUSTRATIONS

BLACK AND WHITE FIGURES

FIGURE 0.1   Disappeared flyer   xx

FIGURE 0.2   Feminicidio graph   xxi

FIGURE 1.1   Government shooting range   30

FIGURE 1.2   Deserted colónia of Guadalupe   41

FIGURE 2.1   Dwellings in Lomas de Poleo   53

FIGURE 3.1   Government feminicidio monument plaque   73

FIGURE 3.2   Pink crosses   76

FIGURE 3.3   Painting the riverbed   80

FIGURE 3.4   Missing poster advertisement   84

FIGURE 4.1   Mural of US role in feminicidio   92

FIGURE 4.2   Mural of Monica Alanis   93

FIGURE 4.3   Mural of Karla Castañeda and Cinthia Jocabeth   95

FIGURE 4.4   Mural of Sagrario Gonzalez Flores   97

FIGURE 5.1   Rastreo in Arroyo del Navajo   113

FIGURE 5.2   Possible feminicidio remains   117

COLOR PLATES

Plates follow page 86.

PLATE 1   The historic moment when the International Caravan for Justice culminated in a joint protest at the US–Mexico border bridge

PLATE 2   Pink crosses erected at the entrance of the main highway into Chihuahua

PLATE 3   Feminicidio memorial cross, which stands directly at the US–Mexico border

PLATE 4   Evidence of armed physical government military intimidation, harassment, and surveillance during the rastreo [search]

PLATE 5   "Las Hormigas" ecological toilets

PLATE 6   One of the hidden rooms in one of the bars on the main promenade of Ciudad Juárez where forced prostitution occurs

PLATE 7   The largest cemetery in Ciudad Juárez

PLATE 8   Flyer circulated to publicize the "Arroyo del Navajo" rastreo [Navajo Riverbed search] for victims' remains

PLATE 9   Pink crosses erected by family members at the location of the Arroyo del Navajo [Navajo Riverbed] to mark the mass gravesite of feminicidio remains

PLATE 10   Image of the dancing water fountains installed by the government

PLATE 11   Marking of a site where remains were found during the rastreos [searches] for feminicidio remains in the Arroyo del Navajo [Navajo Riverbed]

PLATE 12   Señor José Luís searching for his daughter

PLATE 13   Evangelina Arce, Mother of Silvia, keeps this collection of her personal artifacts from the movement

ACKNOWLEDGMENTS

THIS BOOK'S attempt to make sense of the feminicidios in Ciudad Juárez and Chihuahua, Mexico, has been a collective process of labor, generosity, and commitment. Throughout the course of my research, I worked with many individuals, families, not-for-profit organizations, NGOs, political groups, activist organizations, and academic institutions.

My home university, Loyola Marymount University (LMU), has supported my work in Juárez since 2003. LMU, in its commitment to social justice, supported my scholar-activist work in numerous ways. LMU has provided me with research, teaching, and travel grants. LMU's Center for Service and Action supported my endeavor to bring students to Juárez to interrogate feminicidio and globalization. LMU also welcomed and provided stipends of support for the Mothers of the feminicidio victims and disappeared, as well as for Juárez artists and activists to come to our campus and share their testimonios and solidarity initiatives. LMU supported two sabbaticals in order for me to write, conduct interviews, translate and transcribe documents, and engage in activism on the border. Particular colleagues at LMU were instrumental in my success at these endeavors: Barbara Busse, Dean Scheibel, Paige Edley, Abhik Roy, Wenshu Lee, Michele Hammers,

Kyra Pearson, JongHwa Lee, Lisa Lugo, Pam Rector, Lorena Chavez, Jessica Viramontes, Judith Scalin, and Keith Bryant Alexander. In addition to my being supported by faculty and staff members, several students over the years served as my Rains Research Assistants on this project. I am indebted to the hard work of Maria Franco-Rahman and Kat Soto-Gómez. I would like to thank my translating and transcribing team, consisting of Maria Scheel, Helga Estrada, and Victor Cruz, for their diligent work and devotion to this project. Of course, I would like to thank all of my students and our student body who participated in the too-many-to-count consciousness-raising events, talks, town halls, protests, and teach-ins on the topic of the Juárez feminicidios.

In addition to the institutional support I received from LMU, throughout the years I have worked with many organizations in Ciudad Juárez. I would like to thank the following activist groups and non-profits for their collaboration, input, and guidance: Nuestras Hijas de Regreso a Casa, Justicia Para Nuestras Hijas, Mujeres de Negro, Amigas de las Mujeres de Juárez, Las Hormigas, Rosas Rojas Juárez, Frenté Marginal, Red Mesa de Mujeres, Casa Amiga, Grupo de Acción por los Derechos Humanos y la Justicia Social, Graffiti Heads Cru, and Mexico Solidarity Network.

In addition to working with specific organizations, I worked very closely with numerous people in developing solidarity initiatives and in support of my specific research. I would like to thank Tom Hansen, Macrina Cardenas, Abi Thornton, Diana Washington Valdez, Veronica Leyva, Felix Pérez, Maclovio Fierro Hurtado Martinez, Lluvia Rocha, Julia E. Monárrez, and Judith Galarza. I would also like to thank Angela Aguayo and Alex Hivoltze-Jimenez, who produced the documentary !Ni Una Más! alongside my own research in an attempt to spread awareness.

Although I interviewed and worked alongside many of the families of the murdered and disappeared, over the years I worked very closely with several of the Mothers, activists, and family members of the feminicidio victims, including Norma Esther Andrade, Malu García Andrade, Paula Flores, Marisela Ortiz, Patricia Cervantes, and Señor Don José Luis.

I would like to thank The Ohio State University Press for their publication and editorial support. I was fortunate enough to have the literal "dream team" of editors for this special series, "New Directions in Rhetoric and Materiality." Editors Barbara A. Biesecker, Wendy S. Hesford, and Christa Teston, every step of the way, provided supportive, critical, and informative feedback to continually push this project forward. I, of course, am particularly indebted to Tara Cyphers, who believed in this project's importance from the very beginning, and in the importance of having the Mothers' stories told. I thank her for her patience, enthusiasm, and careful treatment of this work. In addition to my editorial team, I would like to thank Cynthia Bejarano, who served as one of my unblinded reviewers, and to express my tremendous appreciation to the other, unknown, blind reviewer. Both individuals offered incredibly meticulous feedback. I am indebted to my loving, always supportive, and amazing partner—a theorist and activist extraordinaire—Dana L. Cloud, for her ongoing comradery, guidance, direction, and feedback on my manuscript. It is her work on materiality that inspires my own. She, indeed, is my Marxist muse. I am also grateful for the insightful feedback provided on this project by Mary Triece.

Finally, I am forever grateful for the ongoing love and support from my family members. My children, Dylan, Sarah, and Benjamin Reich, have been my biggest cheerleaders and supporters. Finally, the support from my former partner, Alex Reich, my late papá, Ruben R. Lozano, my mother, Nina Ellen Lozano, my tia Irma Lozano, and my brother, Ruben R. Lozano II, has never wavered.

PREFACE

Feminicidio in Ciudad Juárez

IN 2010, after public outcry, MAC Cosmetics and the fashion brand Rodarte pulled their "Juárez" limited-edition makeup collection and issued a public apology for their cosmetics line's "unfortunate choice of names." MAC and Rodarte intended to capitalize on the sensationalism surrounding the feminicidios—the killing of women and girls in Ciudad Juárez in the early 2000s. The MAC makeup collection, which featured lip glosses, blushes, eyeshadows, and nail polishes, titled "factory," "Juárez," "ghost town," "del Norte," and "quinceanera," was inspired by Rodarte designers Kate and Laura Mulleavey's trip to the "ethereal" US–Mexico border, where they reported being inspired by "the idea of workers in Mexican maquiladoras [factories] walking half-asleep to the factories in Juárez, after dressing in the dark" (as cited in Hing, 2010).

In the early 2000s Ciudad Juárez became known for a string of grisly murders, which were originally articulated as serial killings rather than as a systemic phenomenon (Valdez, 2006). Media hype commonly referred to Juárez as "the feminicidio capital of the world" (Cevallos, 2004), "the capital of murdered women" (Nieves, 2002), and "the most dangerous city in the world" (Bowdon, 1998). Media coverage, primarily from local newspapers in Juárez (*El Diario*) and Chihuahua (*El Norte*), suggested that the killings were targeting a particular population: poor women and young girls between the ages of 15 and 25 years, most often maquiladora workers—many of whom had migrated from other Mexican southern states. In most of these murders, there were signs of sexual violence, abuse, torture—and, in many cases, mutilation (Valdez, 2006). For example, the autopsies often revealed that the women and girls were kept alive for days, tortured with sticks or poles, and had their breasts slashed and nipples removed before being killed. Other women were burned with acid or burning tires and disposed of in cement-filled barrels (E. Cano, personal communication, January 3, 2004). Due to the sensational media coverage of what became known as the "Women of Juárez Murders," theories from journalists, activists, and investigators about the killings began to emerge. The circulation of dominant theories included serial killers, snuff films, human trafficking, organ harvesting, gang initiations, satanic cults, and killings-for-sport by high-powered businessmen and government officials (Valdez, 2006).

In the fall of 2003, UCLA professor Alicia Gaspar de Alba organized a three-day international conference that brought together scholars, students, journalists, artists, activists, authors, and policy specialists, as well as Mothers[1] of the murder victims, in a series of roundtable discussions and presentations to address these theories and to make sense of these gendered crimes. As the event, titled "The Maquiladora Murders, Or, Who Is Killing the Women of Juárez?," was co-sponsored by Amnesty International, the symposium garnered international attention, consequently functioning to spur legal, academic, activist, and popular-culture interventions and responses to the feminicidios in Juárez and Chihuahua. However, as we know, increased visibility in the public sphere does not necessarily translate into liberatory change (Phelan, 1993).

The international explosion of the portrayal of the Juárez feminicidios within popular culture included feature films, art, novels, documentaries, plays, songs, art exhibits, and altáres. Despite widespread recognition of the killings as real, most popular-culture texts about

---

1. Throughout this book, I capitalize the word "mothers" to denote and rhetorically center the Mothers' significant role in leading the global social movement against the feminicidios.

the Juárez feminicidios functioned to perpetuate the feminicidios as myth—or as "a dark legend." For example, Hollywood produced two major motion pictures on the topic. The first, *The Virgin of Juárez,* starring Minnie Driver, contained a supernatural subplot where the "chupacabra," a mythical creature depicted in folklore as killing victims by drinking their blood, was responsible for the murders. *Bordertown,* which starred Jennifer López as an investigative journalist sent to Juárez to uncover the crimes, proposed that human rights activists were responsible for the murders. In addition to the film industry, a plethora of fiction novels were published about the feminicidios (e.g., Agosín, 2006; Ainslie, 2013; Bonasso, 2012; Bowden, 2010a; Duarte, 2008; Gaspar de Alba, 2005; Gibler, 2011; Hawken, 2011, 2013; LaRose, 2015; Lindsay, 2008), with the most popular being Bowden's (2010b) *Murder City.* Taken together, this body of fiction portrayed the women and girls in Juárez as hypersexualized, as weak, and as objects of gratuitous violence.

Not all the cultural artifacts and interventions were inherently mistaken. However, various "critical" interventions were not without controversy. For example, US playwright Eve Ensler, along with American actors Sally Field and Jane Fonda, took *The Vagina Monologues* on the road and performed the play "for" the Mothers in Juárez, in conjunction with several other prominent Mexican actors, in an attempt to draw international attention to the gendered crimes. The Mothers boycotted and walked out of the production because the play offended many of their political and emotional sensibilities. In addition, the Hollywood stars were accused of "stealing the spotlight" for personal gain and of not foregrounding the Mothers in the movement against violence (M. Cardenas, personal communication, November 2004). Mexican supergroups Los Tigres del Norte and Jaguares, along with US superstar Tori Amos, wrote songs about the killings. The Mexican government censored Los Tigres's song "Las Mujeres de Juárez" [The Women of Juárez] from national radio (Cobo, 2004).

Several political interventions had a more efficacious impact on raising awareness about the Juárez feminicidios. Rubén Amavizca's play *Las Mujéres de Juárez,* which is still performed internationally, received critical acclaim and support from many of the Mothers groups for its portrayal of the feminicidios and the social movement. Screenings of

Lourdes Portillo's critical documentary, *Señorita Extraviada* [Missing Young Women], are still being held on college campuses as a form of consciousness-raising about gendered violence.[2]

While the above cultural artifacts were circulating in the public imaginary in the early 2000s, critical academic and activist work on the ground in Ciudad Juárez and Chihuahua had been underway since the early 1990s. For example, in 1993 Julia Monárrez-Fragozo, a professor in Ciudad Juárez at el Colegio de la Frontera Norte, began documenting the feminicidios as a sociopolitical phenomenon with unique characteristics. Similarly, the late Esther Chavez Cano, the founder and director of the first domestic violence center in Ciudad Juárez, Casa Amiga, had begun an archive of every newspaper story published about the killings. In addition to these prominent women, Mothers of the disappeared and murdered women formed their own grassroots groups in Ciudad Juárez and Chihuahua to combat these crimes and fight for justice for their daughters. To borrow Bejarano's (2002) term, the first "Mother-activist" groups to emerge were Voces sin Echo [Voices Without Echo], Nuestras Hijas de Regreso a Casa [May Our Daughters Return Home], and Justicia Para Nuestras Hijas [Justice for Our Daughters]. Another prominent feminist-based organization, Mujeres de Negro [Women in Black], worked closely alongside these "Mother-activist" groups. These organizations collectively make up what is now commonly referred to as the Women of Juárez social movement for justice.

Between 1993 and 2017, 2,381 feminicidios have occurred.[3] As of 2017 in Ciudad Juárez the feminicidios and impunity surrounding these gendered crimes continue. However, the Mexican tourism business, in conjunction with the free-trade maquiladoras [factories], would like the public to think that, like the artifacts that burgeoned in the early 2000s, the feminicidios are a thing of the past. Ciudad Juárez, long referred to as the "most dangerous city in the world," is now being rhetorically constructed as a city that has "left its violent

---

2. See also Steve Hise's *On the Edge: The Feminicidio in Ciudad Juárez* and Angela Aguayo and Alex Hivoltze-Jimenez's *Ni Una Mas / Not One More* documentaries for accurate representations of the Juárez feminicidios.

3. In 2015, there were already 89 feminicidios (Monárrez-Fragoso, 2016), and Justicia Para Nuestras Hijas [Justice for Our Daughters] documented 93 feminicidios in 2016.

past behind" and has "returned to normal." For example, recent headlines read "Once the World's Most Dangerous City, Juárez Returns to Life" (Quinones, 2016), "After Years of Violence, 'Life Is Back' in Juárez" (Valencia, 2015) and "Juárez to Tourists: It's Safe to Come Back Now" (Denvir, 2015). Strikingly, the images that coincide with these headlines include a waterpark, an ice rink, and a zip line. So, while the Mexican government, the tourist industry, and the multinational corporations are depicting business as usual, the 2017 data on the feminicidios and daily militarized violence clearly tells a very different material reality. Murder rates in Juárez, for example, during the period 2016–2017 exceeded 500, the highest murder rate since the height of the "narco wars," over five years ago (Villagran, 2016).[4] Because of this resurgence of violence, as of November 2016 the state had redeployed the military, once again becoming a militarized state.[5] Jessica Morales, a young woman and antifeminicidio activist, explains the current resurgence of Juárez feminicidios and forced disappearances:

> the most alarming [thing] is that we see [missing] posters that are *very* [emphasis in original] recent. We see that they are from *this* very year—from this very month! So what it means is that in Juárez, young women keep on disappearing—every time younger—women as young as 12 years old. (Personal communication, June 24, 2016; emphasis in original)

Not only have the feminicidios not dissipated, the violence in Ciudad Juárez has gotten worse, not better.[6]

---

4. Various factors have given rise to the increase in violence—including the ruling Revolutionary Institutional Party (PRI) being upset by the National Action Party (PAN), narco factions vying for power, and Juárez's Mesa de Seguridad [Network of Security], a security dialogue between authorities and business leaders, being fractured after disagreement on which party to endorse (Corcoran, 2016).

5. The United Nations in November 2016 demanded that Mexico order its military to evacuate amid concerns that once again Mexico as a militarized state would become "permanent or routine" (Román, 2016).

6. The decades of violence in Ciudad Juárez have also had huge psychological impacts on the city's population. According to the Family Centre for Integration and Growth, in collaboration with the Autonomous University of Ciudad Juárez, one in four residents has contemplated taking their own life, and one in 10 has attempted suicide.

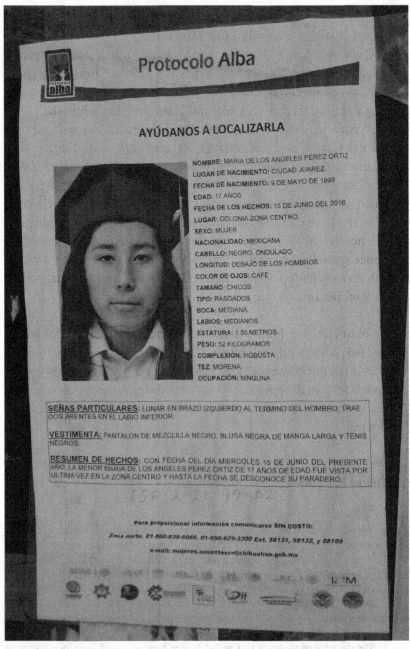

FIGURE 0.1. Disappeared flyer. I took this image of Maria de los Angeles Pérez Ortiz, who went missing on June 15, 2016, the week before I arrived. This image functions as evidence that girls continue to disappear. It also demonstrates the addition of the government's "Alba Protocol." Photo taken by author, Ciudad Juárez, 2016.

FIGURE 0.2. Feminicidio graph. Professor Julia Monárrez-Fragoso has been collecting the most accurate data on the feminicidios since the 1990s: "Base de datos Feminicidio" [archive particular de investigación], Ciudad Juárez, Departamento de Estudios Culturales, Dirección General Regional Noroeste, el Colegio de la Frontera Norte.

Of the 32 countries where feminicidios occur most frequently, 17 are Latin American. Mexico proper, since 2013, has seen a 46 percent rise in feminicidio and is ranked sixth in the world for crimes against women, following Honduras, El Salvador, Argentina, and Guatemala ("Country by Country," 2016).[7] Currently in Mexico, on average, seven women are killed every day—a rate 15 times the world average (Gabor, 2016). Further, the feminicidios, first documented in Ciudad Juárez, began spreading to other regions. In February 2016 government officials in the Mexican state of Jalisco issued a "gender alert" after it was revealed that roughly eight of its municipalities reported a large spike in the number of feminicidios since 2012 ("Mexican State Issues," 2016). Since then, gender alerts have been declared in 41 municipalities, including the states of Morelos, Guerrero, and Michoacán. Furthermore, approximately 20 percent of the country's female population resides in a location where there is an active gender alert ("Gender Alert Declared," 2016). Indeed, across the country of Mexico, according to the "National Citizen Feminicidio Observatory," on average, seven women are killed each day, and often their bodies show evidence of mutilation, torture, and sexual abuse. Of course, due to underreporting, human rights groups recognize that the true numbers are much higher.

DISCURSIVE ATTEMPTS TO ARTICULATE
FEMICIDE/FEMINICIDIO

Because of the uniquely gendered nature of these crimes against women, feminist scholars began attempting to advance a theoretical concept to sufficiently capture the character of these acts. The first attempt at describing the tenets of what constitutes "woman killing by men in a global context" emerged from Jill Radford and Diana Russell's 1992 influential edited volume *Femicide: The Politics of Woman Killing.* Shortly thereafter, Russell's (2001) definition of femicide as "the killing of females by men *because* they are female" (p. 3; emphasis in original) became, and remains today, what constitutes scholarly and legal frame-

---

7. In October 2016 in Argentina, over 10,000 women protested in a day of action against feminicidio. The day of action took place in 138 cities in Argentina, as well as in Chile, Mexico, Uruguay, Bolivia, and the US (Goñi, 2016).

works for interrogating acts of femicide as uniquely gender-specific crimes. Extending theoretical work by Radford and Russell (1992), in a groundbreaking legal move, Catharine MacKinnon (1994), while prosecuting crimes against several survivors of mass killings of Croatian women in the Bosnia–Herzegovina civil war, charged the perpetrators with both genocidal and femicidal practices. In so doing, MacKinnon set the legal stage for interrogating how atrocities against women— whether during war or during peacetime—are wrought with gendered distinctions (Russell, 2001).

Although MacKinnon's (1994) definition carried international legal weight, the growing phenomenon of femicide in Latin America, and in Juárez specifically, necessitated examining the efficacy of the term to describe the crimes. This is because in Spanish, because of the translation process, "femicide" translates to "homicide," generally, which disallows for the gendered nature of the crimes to be sufficiently captured. Thus, in Ciudad Juárez, as well as other Latin American countries such as Guatemala and El Salvador, family members of the disappeared and femicide victims began deploying the terms *femicidio* and *feminicidio* to provide a more culturally specific framework to analyze these crimes. In addition to the term *feminicidio* sufficiently capturing the gendered nature of the killings, scholars Fregoso and Bejarano (2010) argued that the term *feminicidio* simultaneously allowed for categories of analysis that exceed gender. Fregoso and Bejarano (2010) suggested that the concept of feminicidio allows for "a critical transborder perspective . . . rooted in social, political, economic, and cultural inequalities" (p. 4). Guadalupe Morfín, former commissioner for the "Office of the Prevention and Eradication of Violence Against Women in Ciudad Juárez," explained:

> We are all working on this issue because these are new terms used by women to define their problems. *Feminicidio* is defined as an assassination of a woman—specifically. *Feminicidio* also explains the cultural context that these crimes happen under. One of our [office's] points to work on in the future is the concept of *feminicidio,* so we can translate it into legal code. (Personal communication, November 3, 2004)[8]

---

8. As of 2017, *feminicidio* is not yet recognized as a legal category in the state of Chihuahua. This legal deficiency is addressed in the conclusion.

Scholars analyzing the feminicidios in Ciudad Juárez took Fregoso and Bejarano's (2010) call for broader categories of analysis to heart and began attempting to understand the nature of the murders of the women in Juárez from broader theoretical perspectives. The bodies of scholarship examining the feminicidios can be demarcated in the literature by different foci of analysis. One body of work has been devoted to highlighting the transnational feminist and human rights activist forms of resistance against the feminicidios (e.g., Bejarano, 2002; Camacho, 2010; Fregoso, 2006; Fregoso & Bejarano, 2010; Garcia-Del Moral, 2015; Mueller, Hansen, & Qualtire, 2009; López, Caballero, & Rodríguez, 2010; Rojas, 2010; Simmons & Coplan, 2010; Staudt, 2008, 2009a, 2009b; Staudt & Coronado, 2010; E. Wright, 2005; M. Wright, 2010a, 2010b).

Other scholarship has focused on how the feminicidios have been represented through various media and cultural frames within the public sphere (e.g., Blancas, 2010; Bueno-Hansen, 2010; Camacho, 2004; Corona, 2010; Corona & Domínguez-Ruvalcaba, 2010; Driver, 2015; Fregoso, 2000; Harrington, 2015; Holling, 2014; López-Lozano, 2010; M. Wright, 2004). Still other scholarship focused on the feminicidios' relationship to NGOs and legal frameworks (Domínguez-Ruvalcaba and Corona, 2010; Ensalaco, 2006; Iturralde, 2010; Lagarde y de los Ríos, 2010; Luévano, 2012; Pineda-Madrid, 2011; Segato, 2010; Staudt & Coronado, 2002; Weissman, 2010). Investigative journalistic work has also provided research on groups and institutions allegedly responsible for the killings (Rodriguez, Montané, & Pulitzer, 2007; Valdez, 2006).

The final body of work that is most germane to this book's theoretical contributions has focused on the relationship between feminicidio, globalization, and free trade on the US–Mexico border (e.g., Arriola, 2010; Córdoba, 2010; Fragoso, 2003; Gaspar de Alba, 2010; Gaspar de Alba & Guzmán, 2010; Livingston, 2004; Monárrez-Fragoso, 2010; Olivera, 2010; Volk & Schlotterbeck, 2010; Wise, 2006; Wright, 2001a, 2001b). Taken together, this body of work, tapping in to the trope of "disposability," contends that an inherent relationship exists between the killing of women in Ciudad Juárez and a woman's monetary worth within the boundaries of Juárez's neoliberal free-trade zone. In response to these arguments interrogating cultural perceptions of women's worth and neoliberal capitalism, several scholars have critiqued this work and, instead, have argued that these lines of analysis undermine justice

movements' attempts to stop the impunity surrounding the feminicidios, by reifying the inevitability of violence on women's bodies (see
Schmidt Camacho, 2004; Malloy, 2016).

I disagree with Schmidt Camacho (2004) and Malloy (2016). I contend that a turn away from the question of what material forces "make"
the women of Juárez disposable obfuscates attention to the structural
hegemonic forces which give rise to feminicidio in the first place. Consequently, a turn back to the material is warranted.

INTRODUCTION

New Materialism and
Border Materialism

SINCE THE inception of the aforementioned work published on the feminicidios concerning material economic forces and women's disposability, scholarship on mattering and materiality has proliferated. However, scholars attempting to theorize the materiality of the killings have not yet tapped into this nascent body of work (e.g., Arriola, 2010; Córdoba, 2010; Fragoso, 2003; Gaspar de Alba, 2010; Gaspar de Alba & Guzmán, 2010; Livingston, 2004; Monárrez-Fragoso, 2010; Olivera, 2010; Volk & Schlotterbeck, 2010; Wise, 2006; Wright, 2001a, 2001b). Further, previous theorizing on feminicidio and materiality has been inadequate in helping us fully understand how the cultural and neoliberal forces work to produce feminicidio. Thus, marrying the questions currently put forth in theories of *new materialism,* alongside the questions of economic materialism's relationship to the killing and disappeared women in Juárez, affords us a unique opportunity to interrogate some of the key premises of the new materialist turn while examining the feminicidios in new ways. This book seeks to accomplish two things. First, it offers a theoretical corrective to the posthumanistic turn through the advancement of a new theoretical frame: *border mate-*

rialism.[1] Second, it sheds light on the neoliberal material properties that function to produce feminicidio. In so doing, this project not only offers important theoretical contributions to questions concerning the relationship between rhetoric and materiality proper but also assists scholar-activists attempting to intervene in the movement to end the impunity surrounding these gendered crimes.

THEORETICAL DEBATES ON MATERIALITY

Before laying out the tenets of new materialism, a brief historical overview of the various theoretical iterations of materialism is necessary. Several theoretical trajectories on materiality studies continue to be centered and debated in the field of communication studies. The first line of inquiry contends that materiality should be squarely grounded in the tenets of historical Marxism (e.g., Cloud, 1994, 2006; Cloud & Gunn, 2011; Cloud, Macek, & Aune, 2006). The second trajectory, influenced by work by Althusser (1971), Foucault (1980), and Laclau and Mouffe (1985), suggests that discourse attains its materiality through processes of interpellation, representation, and constitutive properties (e.g., Bost & Greene, 2011; Greene, 1998, 2004, 2006, 2010; Gronbeck, 2009; McGee, 1982). Recently, in response to a special issue of *Communication and Critical Cultural Studies,* celebrating Greene's (1988) National Communication Association's Charles H. Woolbert Research Award, a slew of essays (e.g., Greene, 2015; May, 2015; Schiappa, 2015; Sloop, 2015; Swenson, 2015) have turned the attention back to this second trajectory, which builds upon the discipline of rhetoric's recent embrace of the new materialist turn.

New Materialist Turn

Recently, a new line of scholarship has flourished regarding the role of matter, and mattering. Following the influential work of Barad's *Meeting the Universe Halfway* (2007) and Bennett's *Vibrant Matter* (2010), a body of scholarly work produced by rhetorical, feminist, and political

---

1. I thank Dr. Dana L. Cloud for the thoughtful discussions in helping to articulate this theoretical frame.

theorists has taken what is now commonly referred to as the new materialist/posthumanistic turn. This transdisciplinary turn is ripe with new theoretical questions that have important implications for how we think about past and current debates on material and discursive phenomena. Beginning with the premise that post-Marxist and poststructuralist theorizing rooted in notions of social construction has been exhausted—and has run up against limits in attempting to grapple with current pressing questions such as bio- and geopolitics—scholars have returned to projects recentering the role of the material.

For instance, Hennessey (1993) points to a building of scholarly frustration with a privileging of the linguistic:

> A rigorous materialist theory of the body cannot stop with the assertion that the body is always discursively constructed. It also needs to explain how the discursive construction of the body is related to nondiscursive practices in ways that vary widely from one social formation to another. (p. 46)

The new materialist turn is most often articulated as "new materialism," "new material feminisms," and/or "onto-epistemology" (e.g., Ahmed, 2010; Alaimo & Hekman, 2008; Barad, 2007; Barla, 2016; Barnett & Boyle, 2016; Bennett, 2010; Braidotti, 2010; Cheah, 2010; Chow, 2010; Clare, 2016; Colebrook, 2008; Connolly, 2010; Coole, 2010; Coole & Frost, 2010; Edwards, 2010; Frost, 2010; Gabrielson, 2016; Grosz, 2010; Harris, 2015; Kruks, 2010; Meibner, 2016; Orlie, 2010; Pflugfelder, 2016; Pitts-Taylor, 2016; Rickert, 2013; Washick & Wingrove, 2015; Wirth-Cauchon, 2016). These new materialist ontologies emerge, at this historical moment, grounded in the theoretical premise that suggests that historical materialism is too reductionistic and mechanistic, on the one hand, yet expressing a frustration with the poststructuralist/linguistic turn that is perceived as placing too much emphasis on discursive constructions, on the other. Influenced by the work of Grosz (1994), who posited that the body and biology are nonreductionist and full of possibility, coupled with Haraway's (2008) articulation of the "material-semiotic" in the cyborg, Barad (2007) extends these themes in her work by contending that "matter and meaning are not separate elements. They are inextricably fused together, and no event, no matter how energetic, can tear them asunder" (p. 3).

Barad (2003), moreover, suggests that because of this inextricability, *neither* [emphasis added] the discursive nor the material should be *privileged* [emphasis added] when engaging in analyses of matter:

> The relationship between the material and the discursive is one of mutual entailment. Neither is articulated/articulable in the absence of the other; matter and meaning are mutually articulated. Neither discursive practices nor material phenomena are ontologically or epistemologically prior. Neither can be explained in terms of the other. Neither has privileged status in determining the other. (p. 822)

As such, Barad (2003) contends, the material and the discursive should not be viewed as dichotomous. She advances the notion of "material-discursive phenomena" as a way "out" of this theoretical conundrum:

> All bodies, not merely "human" bodies, come to matter through the world's iterative intra-activity—its performativity. This is true not only of the surface or contours of the body but also of the body in the fullness of its physicality, including the very "atoms" of its being. Bodies are not objects with inherent boundaries and properties; they are material-discursive phenomena. (p. 823)

Tenets of New Materialism

New materialists' escape from what is viewed as an untenable theoretical problematic can be partitioned into three distinct themes: "agentic thing power," "assemblages of object-oriented things," and "vibrant enchanted matter." In advancing these theoretical frames, new materialists seek to grant "vitality to nonhuman bodies, forces, and forms . . . expos[ing] a wider distribution of agency," thereby tightening the puppet strings of the "fantasies of human mastery" (Bennett, 2010 p. 122). This posthumanist anthropomorphic turn replaces human agency with "assemblages" and posits "nonhuman materialities as actors" (Bennett, 2005, p. 446).

Bennett's (2015) work on "vibrant matter," for example, also referred to as the study of "object-oriented things," advances a posthumanist paradigm where matter contains its own agentic properties. This approach calls for scholars to address the "agency of human and *non-*

human assemblages" (p. 445; emphasis added). Barad (2007) contends that things have agentic qualities: things "kick back" at human agents— they possess "thing power." Bennett (2015) turns to the tropes of "wonder" and "enchantment" when attempting to theorize "thing power." Barnett and Boyle (2016) and Pflugfelder (2015) offer the "thing power" of speed bumps and beer hops, respectively, to make a case for how things impact movement, bodies, and outcomes in the public sphere.

Bennett (2015) elaborates on the agentic qualities of these types of things in her label "thing-power." The types of things that Bennett (2015) is enchanted with, in her writings, include a dead rat, a plastic cap, and a spool of thread. Bennett (2010) writes:

> For had the sun not glinted on the black glove, I might not have seen the rat; had the rat not been there, I might not have noted the bottle cap, and so on. But they *were* [emphasis in original] all there just as they were, and so I caught a glimpse of an *energetic vitality* [emphasis added] inside each of these things. (p. 5)

Bennett's work (2010), perhaps sensing an impending critique of this posthuman turn, doubles down on the vibrancy of things: "I believe it is wrong to deny vitality to nonhuman bodies, forces, and forms, and that a careful course of anthropomorphizing can help reveal that vitality" (p. 122). Extending Bennett's (2010) formative work, Barnett and Boyle's (2016) edited volume also argues for the vibrant matter of things. Their essays include analyses of the agentic nature of bicycles, refrigerators, phones, keyboards, and washing machines, among others.

Posthumanist Critique

I contend that the posthumanistic new materialist turn is fraught with dangers in its disavowal of human agency, in its complicity with neoliberal capitalism, and through its fetishization of objects-oriented things. Moreover, I argue that if current scholarly endeavors adopt this new materialist orientation, this will result in an ontologically flattened move, whereby political action is disarmed. However, that is not to say that we should throw the baby out with the bathwater. *What* new materialist theories have been focusing on—objects, matter, as well as the assemblages of things—all play a critical role in helping scholars understand the material forces that give rise to various cultural crises—such as feminicidio. Indeed, the aforementioned studies within this new materialist turn are taking up critical issues such as the environment, sustainability, production, genetics, disease, and biopolitics. These are undeniably some of the most urgent political questions of our time. Yet, new materialism's decentering of the human subject risks rendering unintelligible the ways that individuals and groups working within systems of power communicate and interrelate, within their lived conditions, in collective struggle for social change. To avoid these perils, I argue for a resuscitation of historical materialism and dialectics that enable a more critical understanding of the assemblages of things while making room for the role of human agency for political projects.

Historical materialism has never wavered in its focus on the situated, contextual, and historical nature of material conditions rooted in struggle. As Roy and Subramaniam (2016) point out, "perhaps [new materialism] improperly and too quickly buried many . . . old 'bodies' [of scholarship] and exhumed a new 'body' that is not entirely feminist or even particularly new" (p. 23). And yet, throughout much of the new materialist body of scholarship, historical materialism acts as the implicit straw argument, often implied as that which new materialism positions itself against (e.g., Ahmed, 2010; Alaimo & Hekman, 2008; Barad, 1998, 2003, 2007, 2008; Barla, 2016; Barnett & Boyle, 2016; Bennett, 2010, 2015; Braidotti, 2010; Cheah, 2010; Chow, 2010; Clare, 2016; Colebrook, 2008; Connolly, 2010; Coole, 2010; Coole & Frost, 2010; Frost, 2010; Gabrielson, 2016; Grosz, 2010; Harris, 2015; Kruks, 2010; Meibner, 2016; Orlie, 2010; Pflugfelder, 2015, 2016; Pitts-Taylor, 2016; Rickert, 2013; Washick & Wingrove, 2015; Wirth-Cauchon, 2016). In opposition to the new materialist theorizing of the material, I argue that not all forces or effects operate in equal fashion. Moreover, human and nonhuman entities and interactions are always imbedded in structures of power and necessity. A historical dialectical positioning understands human agency as situated within a particular historical moment with an ontology necessary to attribute meanings objects to things, and to use those material elements for a strategic purpose. Without this ontology, a new materialist's decentering of the human subject in the name of an underdetermined false equivalence runs the risk of resulting in epistemological distortion and political ineptitude.

In formulating this theoretical corrective, my project, when analyzing the material properties of feminicidio, strengthens and engages concepts central to the rhetorical tradition that are severely crippled by the new materialist shift. These concepts include the notion of collective struggle, civic engagement, strategies of resistance, and justice projects focused on the common good; these projects stand in direct opposition to new materialism's emphasis on the self and on individual, rather than societal, responsibility. In addition, historical materialism grants that individuals are fashioned and influenced by effects on bodies that can be comprehended by an "object existing outside it, indispensable to its integration and the expression of its essential being" (Marx, 1844/1978, p. 116). Recentering human agency need not result in the enacting of the all-knowing rational subject but, instead, acknowledges as the starting point that humans are "real, corporeal," standing "with feet firmly on the solid ground" (Marx, 1844/1978, p. 115). Historical materialism refocuses attention on human struggle, in relation to the material, with all of its desires, complexities, and constrictions.

Perhaps most important to my thesis that feminicidio is produced and fueled by neoliberal capitalist social relations is the effort of projects like this to reassert the notion of a material reality understood as existing in a dialectical relationship with discursive phenomena. The Juárez feminicidios must be viewed in a twenty-first-century neoliberal context in which they reside—a context marked by gross disparities in wealth and by human despair. Those of us committed to critical scholarship have a moral obligation to interrogate systems and structures of power and hegemony, rather than dismissing these systems as "targets of blame." Bennett (2015), when defending the posthumanist turn, states, "What is lost in the move from historical to new materialism . . . is the satisfaction of having a root cause that is targetable and blame worthy" (p. 87). There is a root cause of the feminicidios in Ciudad Juárez, and that root cause *is* neoliberal capitalism. Not only should neoliberal capitalism be blamed and targeted, it must be attended to— in every facet of its power and properties. It must be called out and resisted for its direct role in producing, perpetuating, and sustaining the feminicidios of the women of Juárez.

Border Materialism as a New Direction

What is needed, then, is a new theoretical framework that affords scholars a space to speak about objects, things, and matter that retains the element of human agency, attunes carefully to the role of economic and cultural forces, and yet focuses on the importance of physical matter and the assemblages of things in relation to cultural phenomena—in this case, the Juárez feminicidios. I call this theoretical framework *border materialism*. Border materialism is a theoretical framework that offers scholars a lens to examine how object-oriented things and matter intersect with bodies—in particular, women's bodies—rooted in neoliberal economic structures within specific geographical boundaries mediated by human agency for political change.

In addition to acting as a theoretical corrective to theories of new materialism, border materialism attends to the material properties that produce feminicidio on the US–Mexico border. Border materialism, like the US–Mexico border, straddles both elements of new materialist thought and historical materialism and provides a new specific framework with which to examine the feminicidios as they are produced within the US–Mexico free-trade zones driven by a neoliberal capitalist logic. Border materialism develops upon the understanding of both traditions by asking scholars to look at the feminicidios in Ciudad Juárez through their specific structural, geopolitical, cultural, and economic properties. The feminicidios are not perpetuated by a person; they are perpetuated by and through a system of US–Mexico border relations of violent productions. Neoliberal capitalism is omnipresent. These violent productions, produced by the maquiladoras, are deposited in what is perceived as a "wasteland" on the US–Mexico border, with no regard for the life forces that must dwell and survive in these conditions. Border materialism provides a methodological framework to focus on the *processes* by which feminicidios are produced in relation to how women's bodies border objects and matter. Bodies are always on the periphery, encircled and surrounded by the material properties wherein they reside.

The analytical charge of border materialism encourages scholars to examine the killings of women in an intersectional fashion in relation to the inseparable narco wars, the corrupt state of Chihuahua and the Mexican government, the US–Mexico free-trade agreements, the militarization of the border, and the cultural, political, and economic conditions that women's bodies inescapably border and brush up against daily. Border materialism addresses the inadequacies of new materialist thought by recasting the tenets of new materialist thought in a new direction—one that concretely centers women's oppression, positions the human as the agent in the context of neoliberal capitalism, and thereby offers a more nuanced way of understanding the relationship between object-oriented things and women's oppression in their current historical application.

In taking up the new materialist focus of object-oriented things through the advancing of this new theoretical frame, I answer the call of Coole and Frost (2010) in their edited collection *New Materialisms: Ontology, Agency, and Politics* for scholars examining the new materialist turn to put forth "new concepts and theoretical frameworks in order to understand the complexities of global capitalism (in its broadest sense) and its diverse, localized efforts on everyday lives" (p. 25). This book embodies instantiations of border materialism through each chapter's "taking up" of the key tenets of the posthumanist turn, such as "objects," "assemblages of things," "thing power," and "vibrant matter," in relation to the impact of globalization on women's bodies in this border town. In so doing, this book's chapters act as distinct, yet always interconnected, case studies, demonstrating both the limits and the possibilities of the new materialist turn while interrogating the systems and structures that produce and perpetuate feminicidio.

METHODOLOGICAL APPROACHES
Scholar-Activist Subject Position

Before proceeding to the chapter outline, I situate my scholarly and political relationship to this project. My work began by attempting to study feminicidio through "the material and discursive histories of communities outside of academe" (Coogan & Ackerman, 2010, p. 1). Since 2003 I have been studying and engaging in activism against the feminicidios in Ciudad Juárez and Chihuahua, Mexico. All data in subsequent chapters stems from my relationships formed with the Mothers, family members, and activists in Juárez and Chihuahua over the last 15 years. Further, data analyzed in this book stems from my personal collection of movement artifacts, as well as archival work conducted at New Mexico State University's "Esther Chavez Cano Collection" of feminicidio documents. All public discourse analyzed throughout this book's chapters were audio- and video-recorded by me at various town halls, symposia, protests, marches, and rallies. All visual images provided in this book were photographed by me while I participated as a scholar-activist in various political events and government meetings—both in the United States and in Mexico.

In my role as a scholar-activist, I have participated in three formal delegations to Juárez, including the 2004 International Caravan for Justice. In 2005 I designed an "alternative break trip" to Ciudad Juárez and Chihuahua, where students and I would listen, learn, and work alongside family members and activists in their struggles for justice against feminicidio. These alternative break programs occurred annually during the period 2005–2008. Over the years, I also brought Mothers of femicide victims and of the disappeared to Los Angeles for speaking engagements to raise public awareness and to garner international involvement and support. I have engaged in protests for justice against the Mexican government—both in the United States and in Mexico. In 2009, due to the rise of the Juárez narco wars and the US State Department's travel warning issues, my home university prohibited my travel to Ciudad Juárez. Therefore, it was not until 2016 that I was able to physically return with university monetary and scholarly support.

Because I felt it vital to return to Juárez to seek unanswered questions and to close the research loop, as it were, I returned to Juárez in June 2016. At this time I participated with victims' family members and activists in the painting of crosses where feminicidio bodies have been found, worked collaboratively in the painting of a mural of one of the disappeared—Maria Elena, participated in numerous protests against the Mexican government and its officials, and interviewed family members and activists. In September 2016 I was invited back by family members and activists to participate in a *rastreo* [search] for victims' remains in the Arroyo del Navajo [Navajo Riverbed].

Although I am conversant in Spanish, I am not fluent. Thus, all the interviews and recordings that I collected and conducted throughout the years were both translated and transcribed by various research assistants who are fluent in Spanish. In total, excerpts from 423 pages of transcripts are integrated throughout this book's chapters. I firmly believe that any proposed political activism or academic solutions to the question of feminicidio must originate from the family members and community activists *themselves*. Thus, while still attending to scholarly questions of new materialism and previously published work on the Juárez feminicidios, I have attempted to privilege the testimony from the Juárez families and activists as much as feasible when generating analysis. Therefore, my theoretical inclinations and argumentative positions are driven directly by the Juárez families' and activists' political sensibilities.

Finally, throughout my years of research, I was told countless times by numerous Mothers and family members of the disappeared and murdered women and girls that many academics were literally "profiting off of their daughters' deaths." Moreover, I was told that many academics would come to Juárez, collect their data, and never return. My commitment to studying, analyzing, organizing, protesting, and teaching about the Juárez feminicidios has never wavered. And it never will. I publish this book with the encouragement and blessing of the family members and activists in Ciudad Juárez whose testimonies are included in this project, and I hope that this book, which is indeed a labor of love—but even more a labor of political commitment—does the family members, the victims, and the movement justice.

Rhetoric in "the Field"

This book functions as a concrete example of attempting to do the "public work of rhetoric" and a turn to engaging the material aspects of rhetoric in "the field." Indeed, as Coogan and Ackerman (2010) contend, and I agree, the public work of rhetoric "is not shaped in our treatises and classrooms alone but in the material and discursive histories of communities outside of academe" (p. 1). As a scholar-activist, I ascribe to nascent work on methodological approaches to participatory rhetorical advocacy where the scholar-activist engages with community members to engage in "the purposeful expression of a subjective construction of reality, utilized for social change, the recognitions of identity, or resisting power structures . . . and may carry strong commitments to democratic processes or a belief in radical advocacy" (Hess, 2016, p. 89). Throughout each chapter, my work elucidates the turn towards this public work of rhetoric and the importance of doing rhetorical projects in "the field"—"the nexus where rhetoric is produced, where it is enacted, where it circulates, and, consequently, where it is audienced" (McKinnon, Asen, Chávez, & Howard, 2016, p. 4).

This is because my rhetorical fieldwork throughout this book is situated in places and spaces such as within the NAFTA free-trade boundary zone, inside the maquiladoras, in the valleys where the feminicidio remains are discarded, in the streets where the marches, rallies, and protests are held, in the shopping districts where the disappeared flyers are posted, in the red-light district where forced prostitution occurs, in spaces of public memorializing, and in the government buildings where policy and protest are rendered visible. In moving my body throughout these sites, I am able to make "embodied judgements" about the Juárez feminicidios (Hess, 2016, p. 87). My work illustrates the necessity of practices of rhetorical inquiry that embody "the field" in order to analyze the "combination of material and discursive constraints that imbue delimited places with meaning and power, but also to how the field is a rhetorical place that acts with, against, and alongside the rhetorical practices it hosts" (Senda-Cook, Middleton, & Endres, 2016, p. 24).

Indeed, when attempting to analyze how material structures produce feminicidio, I contend that it is necessary for the critic to confront the very places and spaces where the material acts of violence occur. My work, then, functions as evidence for the claim that "amid the current groundswell of critical investigation into the rhetoricity of bodies, places, affects, and sensations—topics that often intersect with materiality—we suggest that the field in which rhetoric happens is a significant factor in the material experience of rhetoric" (Senda-Cook et al., 2016, p. 38). As such, I assert that when attending to the material aspects of rhetoric, being in the field where rhetoric happens is not only, as suggested, a "significant factor" but should be adopted as a scholarly commitment and *necessity* when attempting to render sense-making of the material nature of the object of study.

In thinking about how my work can extend discussions on how we, in the academy, do the public work of rhetoric in "the field," I believe that it is critical that we, as "experts," defer to the community members or interlocutors that we are working with. As scholar-activists, we should be striving for what de Onís (2016) refers to as "co-presence" alongside community members. Thus, in each of these chapters, my voice and body's presence is always side by side with the Mothers and activists in Ciudad Juárez. This methodologically embraced co-presence affords readers a layered and rich accounting of the symbolic and material spaces where the feminicidios reside.

Rhetorical Constraints and Opportunities in "the Field"

It is also important for activist-scholars not to romanticize "the field." There are many material constraints upon academics' bodies when attempting to do rhetorical work in the field. These constraints are compounded when attempting to do rhetorical fieldwork that crosses boundaries and borders—both literally and figuratively. For example, although my body has the privilege of being marked as a US scholar-activist when doing research in Ciudad Juárez, what I discovered very shortly after engaging in the International Caravan for Justice was that it was against the Mexican constitution to engage in any form of activism if one is not a Mexican citizen. Thus, in the early 2000s I began the process of applying for dual citizenship. I was eligible for dual citizenship because I am a first-generation US citizen, and my father immigrated to the US, from Mexico, in 1964. I found a way to legitimize my activism. At the same time, by invoking a Mexican passport, I would not be afforded the same rights and protections as a US citizen and researcher if arrested, and so forth. Ultimately I felt that the need to speak out and protest against the feminicidios was paramount. Another constraint on doing work in the field was, of course, the ongoing surveillance and harassment by the state.

Although it is necessary to present my ethos pertaining to my work in Juárez, it is just as imperative to note that my identity as a scholar-activist, in relation to this work, is always and already an "outsider within" (Hill Collins, 1986). No matter how much time I have spent in "the field," attempting to achieve a "standpoint" or a "bifurcated consciousness," to use Harding's (1991) term, my knowledge and experiences are ultimately always incomplete, imperfect, and limited. Similarly, as that of a US scholar-activist, my role is always and already privileged; I am able to vacillate—to come and go across and between borders at will.

With these premises in mind, thus far, current theorizing of "the field" constructs it as an already-existing place and space to conduct rhetorical fieldwork. I contend that scholar-activists engaging in rhetorical fieldwork should consider how we can *create* the field if it currently does not exist. For example, my collection of public testimonies and recorded activities from the antifeminicidio movement in the early 2000s to the present came from working collaboratively with family members and activists on the ground to put together international programming, such as speaking tours, protests, teach-ins, art installations, and delegations, that would create the opportunity for solidarity initiatives. The field we created consisted of governmental meetings, protests, town halls, meetings with not-for-profit organizations, rastreos [searches for remains], testimonio, and question-and-answer sessions with family members of the feminicidio victims and the disappeared. These alterative break trips and delegations were mutually beneficial, as our students were able to learn about the US–Mexico border conditions, while the Juárez activists and family members had the opportunity to circulate their stories to wider publics.

Other examples in thinking about the rhetorical canon of invention in relation to the methodological process of scholar-activists' creating the field can be found in the examples of entering the space of the maquiladora sector as well as climbing Cuernos de la Luna, the mountainous site where Neyra Azucena's body was found. In the first example, because we knew that we would be prohibited entrance into a maquiladora if we presented ourselves as Jesuit social justice students interrogating the oppressive labor conditions of the maquiladoras, we presented ourselves as students of business, interested in learning how to profit, as future business owners, by using the loopholes of the US–Mexico free-trade agreement of NAFTA. We were granted entrance to several Juárez maquiladoras and were able to see the working conditions firsthand, speak with workers to collect their stories, and collect observational data on the lived conditions of many of the factory workers.

In another instance, to demonstrate the government's inane story of how Neyra Azucena's killer carried her lifeless body to the top of Cuernos de la Luna, we accompanied several of Neyra's family members on a two-hour hike up the mountain. Through this process of hiking the mountain, in "the field," the students and I were able to viscerally understand how no one would be physically able to carry a body up the steep and precarious cliffs within a 30-minute period, which was the government's story. When we reached the top of the mountain, Neyra's Mother, Patricia, was able to show us where the narco government's helicopter pad was located—her theory as to how the government disposed of Neyra's body in such a short time. We were also able to physically be in the space where Neyra's body was found, which we learned was a plot of Mexican military land—complete with cameras and security equipment. These experiences in "the field" were not pre-given but rather were created opportunities to engage in research in the field as a collaborative inventive between me and the family members of the victims. Thus, rhetorical scholar-activists should conceive of "the field" as an open set of possibilities that are not predetermined but arise out of rhetorical exigencies to achieve scholar-activist goals.

In summation, I do not believe that being "in the field" is the sufficient standard by which material projects should be measured or evaluated for what constitutes the public work of rhetoric. Instead, in attempting to push the canon, and the work that we do as rhetoricians committed to projects of social justice, I argue that as scholar-activists we must not just analyze but also *act*. I believe that methodical approaches to doing rhetorical fieldwork contain a moral obligation to work with communities toward efficacious and just social change. Thus, each of my chapters should be read as examples of co-presence in the field—not only as sites of analysis but as sites of co-constructed sites of resistance, in attempts to *enact* material change, in real time, as the feminicidios continue to swell around us.

CHAPTER OVERVIEWS

Chapter 1, "Waves of Feminicidio," traces the history of the Juárez and Chihuahua, Mexico, feminicidios from the early 1990s to the present. This chapter demarcates four distinct historical waves of feminicidio. In so doing, it provides all the vital historical events and movement gains in order to gauge the subsequent chapters' theoretical arguments pertaining to the struggles surrounding the feminicidios. Chapter 1 functions as a historical archive of all the material and symbolic events surrounding the feminicidios in Ciudad Juárez. As such, it is an important historical and political resource for scholar-activists.

Chapter 2, "Feminicidio and the 'Enchanted' Assemblages of Things," provides an in-depth analysis regarding the link between the neoliberal capitalist policies of free trade and the feminicidios of the border town of Ciudad Juárez. Troubling the new materialist concept of "the assemblages of things," I demonstrate how the NAFTA-driven maquiladora things on the assembly lines, in conjunction with the assemblage of things in the multinational free-trade zones, have a direct correlation with the feminicidios of the women of Juárez. The assemblages of things analyzed in this chapter include mechanical parts, machinery, pregnancy sticks, feminine pads, roads, buses, sidewalks, lights, and sanitation. I end this chapter with a focus on how the *re*assemblages of things can be deployed as strategies of resistance to neoliberal logics.

In chapter 3, "Feminicidio, Public Memory, and 'Thing Power,'" theories of new materialism are brought into conversation with public memory studies. This chapter juxtaposes an analysis of the Mexican government's hegemonic memorial to the feminicidio victims against the rhetorical efficacy of the activists' own erection of public monuments, with tools that I call "matter-memory-makers." I also reveal how the family members' and activists' strategic "reassemblages of things" function as "practiced matter," working to disrupt dominant logics of the state. Objects of analysis in this chapter include telephone poles, rocks, walls, shopping directories, park benches, and trash receptacles.

Chapter 4 is titled "Feminicidio, Objects, and Affect." Using the mural project "Faces of Feminicidio" as a text, I demonstrate how objects must be given their affective properties through rhetorical mediation. I first provide a history of the mural project in relation to the feminicidios. Next, using Gordon's (2008) theorizing of "haunting," infused by Levinas's (1985) ethics of "the face," I enact a critical reading of how the affective properties of the murals "haunt" the state and public imaginary, thus countering the state's "percepticide" of the feminicide victims while simultaneously promulgating public members to act. Next, by interrogating the murals' placements and tactile relationships to bodies, I theorize what I call "object-oriented affect." Objects of focus in this chapter include spray-paint cans, brushes, concrete, dwellings, and walls.

Chapter 5, "Lifeless or 'Vibrant Matter'?," analyzes the rastreos that are conducted by victims' family members and activists in their ongoing searches for their family members' DNA remains and for the disappeared. This chapter provides a pointed critique of the tropes of "wonder" and "enchantment," which drive much of new materialist scholarship's theoretical orientation. I demonstrate in this chapter how the properties of nonhuman actants must not be theorized as inherently vibrant, as they are always mediated through systems of power. Matter analyzed in this chapter includes shovels, picks, whistles, gloves, plastic bags, clothing, bones, and DNA.

The conclusion chapter makes concrete recommendations, based on field interviews conducted with family members and activists, for addressing the ongoing impunity surrounding the feminicidios in Ciudad Juárez and Chihuahua, Mexico, moving forward. The chapter concludes with a summary of the book's key theoretical contributions and a call for scholar-activists to adopt a new direction in studies of materiality—that of *border materialism*.

CHAPTER 1

Waves of Feminicidio

BEFORE WE TURN to the various case studies that seek to interrogate the efficacy of the dominant theoretical tenets of new materialist inclinations, it is first necessary to historicize the feminicidios in their historical evolution leading up to today's political context. Based on my interviews and analysis of the discourses of the Mothers of the feminicidio victims in relation to the hegemonic strategies and tactics of the Mexican government, I demarcate four distinct historical waves of violence that lay the foundation for the subsequent chapter analyses. Importantly, this chapter, through its historical tracing, also stands alone as a historical archive and resource for scholars studying the phenomenon of feminicidio in Mexico. The following historical litany begins with Wave One.

WAVE ONE: 1993–1998

Wave One of the feminicidios in Ciudad Juárez begins in the early 1990s. During this first wave, scholars, activists, and family members of the murdered and disappeared attempted to "make sense" of the killings. Activist groups were formed in the first attempt to name, make visible, and demand public and government attention to the phenomenon that was occurring. Early movement groups attempted to shed light on the killings and began pressuring for systemic change. Initially, movement was sparked by shared palpable cultural sentiment that "something very wrong" was occurring in Ciudad Juárez:

> In the beginning of the barbarity appeared the first signs that "something" was happening. This is when the public first began hearing about the disappearances of several women, many of them minors— and then with horror, began to discover the first bodies—mutilated, raped, and finally thrown into garbage cans or abandoned. During the early years, the authorities did not try to understand the dimensions of the social phenomenon that was beginning. They did not investigate and try to find and punish the guilty. The authorities also blamed the women "culpándolas" for their own misfortune. The authorities would use phrases like: "why were you dressed like that?" and "what were they doing all alone at night?" It was also common that officials would claim that women were "living a double life." Due to the incompetence and the onslaught of dismissal by public authorities, the first organizations for the defense of the rights of women, which were headed by Mothers, appeared. The Mothers were desperate to find their daughters. It was simply the union of several Mothers, focusing their struggles initially in the pursuit of their daughters, demanding that justice prevail, due to the desire and longing of finding them alive. With regard to the social organizations, the first was led by Judith Galarza and Paula Flores. Their group was titled Voces sin Echo [Voices without Echo]. (Ortiz, 2016)

In addition to Voces sin Echo, in 1997 Mujeres de Negro de Chihuahua [Women in Black] was formed. As one of the founding members recalls: "We formed in 1997. The group's initial goal was to eradicate violence against women. We worked to promote policies for women and to promote legal change. We have worked to denounce violence. We began the chant '¡Ni Una Más!' [Not One More!]" (L. Castro, personal communication, November 3, 2004).

WAVE TWO: 1998–2010

The second wave of violence is operationalized by the decidedly increased international media attention to the gendered crimes, the multiplication of grassroots antifeminicidio groups, and an increasing body of scholarly work turning its attention towards the feminicidios in Ciudad Juárez. Of note, during this wave, a consciousness began to emerge connecting the feminicidios to the larger neoliberal economic structures of Juárez. Ultimately, a clear antagonistic relationship between the attempts for systemic change between the Mothers leading the activist groups and the Mexican government took form. The second wave

> started a turbulent time . . . and clear clash between authorities and the groups of Mothers of the victims of violence. We saw the emergence of more and more bodies, and the continuous loss of more young people—mostly poor, many were employees of the maquiladoras, and the ranges of age were very similar. The Mothers were well organized and began to take on greater strength and visibility in the local, state, and national levels. In 2001, we saw the founding of "Nuestras Hijas de Regreso a Casa," by Marisela Ortiz and Rosario Acosta. Mother Norma Andrade was then also incorporated. (Ortiz, 2016)

Norma recounts how she became part of the movement:

> My name is Norma Estela Andrade García. I am president of Nuestras Hijas. They assassinated my daughter [Lilia Alejandra] on the 21st of February of 2001. In light of her murder, one of her teachers [Marisela Ortiz] began writing editorials in a paper about her case. Four young women disappeared around this time. One per week. One was on the 21st of February. One the 23rd of February. One the 7th of March. One the 13th of March—and one the 27th of March. One of the Mothers of the victims, seeing the teacher's editorials, called for help. She called Marisela, and then she called me. (N. Andrade, personal communication, November 2, 2004)

Founding member Marisela Ortiz explains the organic nature of the emergence of this Mothers group:

Our organization really sort of generated itself very spontaneously after the assassination of Lilia Alejandra Garcia, sister of Marilu, and a former student of mine. We began a series of public actions without the intention to begin any type of organization—it was just a response from loved ones to try and generate some kind of response on the part of the government. Little by little these demonstrations began to generate interest among others families who were experiencing similar conditions or situations. That's when we began to formalize our strategies—to formalize our organization to develop goals—and that's when we located our name, "Nuestras Hijas de Regreso a Casa" [Bring Our Daughters Home], because that's what all the Mothers wanted. In a very naive manner, we began to do this kind of social work—to look for justice for these cases. When we found ourselves running around in circles, we decided to take our struggle to Mexico City—to the capital. (Personal communication, November 2, 2004)

Ramona Morales, another original member of Nuestras Hijas, echoes Norma's experience as an activist:

I didn't know that these groups existed. I was surprised, as I didn't know that they knew about my case. I had never begun to struggle out of necessity. I asked for their help because I did not know the city. We met every eight days. We worked to make agreements—to open the cases of our daughters. (Personal communication, November 2, 2004)

The next group that emerged during the second wave, Justicia Para Nuestras Hijas [Justice for Our Daughters], was based in Chihuahua. Alma Gómez,[1] the first leftist woman in the Chihuahua congress, and the founder of El Barzón de Chihuahua, explained the group's history and focus:

---

1. Alma Gómez, at the invitation of Esther Chavez Cano, in 1997, began accompanying the Mothers in their struggle for justice and was one of the first, with Esther, to document the murders of women in Juárez and Chihuahua.

"Justice for Our Daughters" is a group made up of Mothers and family members of young woman who have disappeared or were murdered in Juárez City and Chihuahua. We began in 2002—and one fundamental aspect is that even before the start of the organization, all of our testimonies have been firsthand. When the Mothers can have access to the case files for their own cases, that's when we will be able to prove to Mexico and the whole world what exactly is happening with these cases—the irregularities within the cases that are omitted by authority members. Our principle objectives and activities are: to defend the human rights of the victims and their families, accompany the victims of violence, carry out investigations, document, and conduct field-work—with respect to this, we have systematized and summarized the case files of the Mothers who are part of the organization. We have a database with all of the names and circumstances of the women who have been killed, or have disappeared. And we carry out investigations of press coverage. (Personal communication, November 3, 2004)

As demonstrated by these founding Mothers' recounting, the emergence of these early Mothers groups embodied Antonio Gramsci's notion of the "organic intellectual"—an "ordinary" individual "whose function in society is primarily that of organizing, administering, directing, educating or leading others" (as quoted in Forgacs, 2000, p. 300).

As the Mothers groups gained prominence, as Ortiz (2016) explains, the government began to engage in hegemonic strategies of suppression:

The Mothers, during this time, received many threats. The government was also completely inept at handling the problem—they began attacking the organizations of civil society by continually running smear campaigns against the Mothers. They began scapegoating people for the murders to look like they were solving the crimes. They created offices that did nothing. Impunity was increasingly growing.

As the killings continued, and the impunity persisted, my work began tracing the hegemonic strategies and tactics of the Mexican government that attempted to deflect and silence the struggles of the Mothers and activists to end the feminicidios. Through my analysis of the Mothers' public testimony, in conjunction with the interviews I conducted, the history of the Mexican government's ineptitude and complicity with the feminicidios can be evidenced through the thematization of the following six distinct hegemonic tactics of impunity, which figured prominently during the second wave and continue to this day.

Falsification of Evidence

A common strategy of the state used to deflect negative media attention about the feminicidios has been to hide, falsify, and destroy forensic evidence. As the former director of the Office to Prevent and Eradicate Violence in Ciudad Juárez reported, "One of the problems and one of the main complaints of the families has been the mishandling of the DNA investigations. Sometimes they have had to take three or four tests— sometimes they come back and ask for hair and blood samples because the tests have been lost" (G. Morfín, personal communication, 2007).

For example, Patricia Cervantes, Mother of feminicidio victim Neyra Azucena, was presented with the skull of a 64-year-old man in lieu of her own daughter's remains:

> We don't want people who were negligent, or who may have been an accomplice in this crime. My last step is to exhume her body . . . and to have honest people from abroad . . . to study her body—bone by bone—to assess if it's really my daughter . . . entirely. Because if her skull is missing, then what else? Why? Why? Why are you doing this? You've brought me my daughter twice . . . you first brought me her skull, and now you are bringing me some of her ribs . . . ? I'm missing the rest. How many bones do our bodies have?! How long will I have to wait?! With all of these anomalies, how did you expect me to trust anyone? Why? Because from the beginning, the investigators didn't do their jobs as they should have. (P. Cervantes, personal communication, November 2, 2004)

Harassment

Mothers, in the process of seeking answers about the status of the investigations of their missing daughters, experienced ongoing forms of harassment:

For those who do not know, Alma, Lucha, and Yolanda were given death threats. They have received a couple of death threats over the last couple of years. They were all charged with completely invented crimes by the state attorney general. They were arrested there for a while, and all because they are standing up for women in Juárez and Chihuahua. (T. Hansen, personal communication, January 3, 2005)

Evangelina Arce [Doña Eva], Mother of Silvia, explains the persistent harassment she has experienced over a period of decades:

They continue to send me threats and follow me. I often don't even know if they are the people walking behind, or in front of me . . . some time ago they threatened me to stop talking, or they were going to kill me. I will never shut up—not until my daughter appears, dead or alive. It's been 18 years, and her body hasn't appeared. (Personal conversation, June 27, 2016)

Revolving Door

A state tactic of opening and closing, and switching, government offices has made it impossible for the investigations to move forward. For example, when Ramona, Mother of Silvia, finally met with the governor of Chihuahua, she recounts, "He told me, 'This is not my problem. You should have asked to meet with the previous governor.' He then patted me on my head and said, 'You should go to the federal government.'" Another Mother reported:

On Friday, Irma confronted who the prosecutor of the case was—but she [Suly Ponce] said that it wasn't her responsibility either. When we speak to them [government officials], they send us to the prosecutor so we can try and change the death from suicide to murder. Then the prosecutor tells us that that isn't her responsibility—that we are at the wrong office. So what the hell are we going to do? (Anonymous, personal communication, January 3, 2005)[2]

2. Family members or activists who requested to remain anonymous for safety reasons are cited as "anonymous" throughout this book.

Tactics to Divide the Mothers

During the second wave of feminicidio violence, the government strategy of using material objects and economic resources to divide the Mothers was frequently used. Norma Andrade explains:

> This is the way that the government is able to divide us—because they will help some of us, but not others—so 600,000 pesos—the federal government said they were able to offer as reparations to the victims' families, but the money comes with a lot of conditions. They think this will shut us up, and [make us] argue among ourselves, but it is not going to. (Personal communication, January 4, 2004)

Ramona's testimony also underscores this tactic:

> The government office, the "Chihuahua Institute for Women," has served to manipulate us Mothers. The organization has taken us to meet with Congress, but chooses not to take them [other Mothers]. So, they have helped me, but I still denounce them, because other Mothers are not receiving help. (Personal communication, January 4, 2004)

The Mothers, as highlighted, were able to see through this strategy of the state, and they continued to struggle together.

Quelling "Hysteria"

As the Mothers became more vocal and visible in the public sphere, a dominant strategy was to articulate them as "hysterical" subjects, which "necessitated" private, therapeutic aid. Juanita recounts her testimony of being forcefully committed by the state when she began demanding that the government act: "They [the government] kept telling me I was hysterical. They forced me into a mental hospital. They told me that I needed mental help—that I was not thinking clearly. They put me there two times" (J. Villalobos, personal communication, September 17, 2016).

While Juanita's case of psychological suppression is quite explicit, a subtler, yet equally effective strategy is the "therapeutic" tactics of the state. For example, Vicky Caraveo began "doll therapy" to aid the Mothers in their distress. One activist recounts:

> They would keep the Mothers busy making dolls. They [authorities] didn't even know their [the Mothers'] names. I went to pick up one of the Mothers, and they were all locked in a hotel room! When I asked for the Mother, they didn't even know her name, they [authorities] would say, "You, over there, the one in the back." They were working on dolls for hours and hours—like a sweatshop, and where did the proceeds go? How did it help the movement? (Maclovio, personal communication, June 25, 2016)

As Cloud (1998) has argued, therapeutic discourses act hegemonically by focusing on private and individual solutions rather than social and political systems of power that perpetuate the need for psychological assistance in the first place.

Never Searched / Double Life

One of the most painful tactics identified by the Mothers was the government's refusal to search for their disappeared daughters, or their daughters' remains. Julieta's Mother explains how the authorities did not feel obligated to search for her daughter—and that, instead, they were doing the families of the disappeared "a favor":

> I am Consuelo Valenzuela, Mother of Julieta Marlen González. She disappeared the 7th of March, of 2001, when she was 17 years old. She studied in the high school downtown and worked at a maquiladora. She left school and they saw her standing at the bus stop, and we never knew anything else about her. When our daughters disappeared, the majority were under age. The law states that when this happens the authorities must act out of duty—well, no, they don't look. When we argued this, they told us that the disappearance of someone does not constitute a crime here in Chihuahua, and that if they help us in our search, it's because they are nice and they do it as "social work," not as an obligation. Whatever the case may be, my daughter is lost and the authorities have not looked for her. (C. Valenzuela, personal communication, January 4, 2005)

Authorities would also tell the Mothers that their daughters were living "la double vida" [a double life].[3] One Mother explains her experience when attempting to get the authorities to search for her missing daughter:

I am Hortensia Enriquez, the Mother of Érika Nohemi Carrillo Enriquez. My daughter disappeared on Tuesday the 12th of December, the year 2000, at 6:00 p.m. She left the house with 50 pesos and wearing sandals. She was going to get a haircut at the Multimarket Zarca in the western part of the city, near our colony. When we began meeting with the authorities, they did not have her listed as one of the disappeared, even though my other daughter had reported her missing the day after she did not come home to sleep. The police almost always say that the disappeared "deserved their fate," because they are "bad" people, with habits that are not too good—that they expose themselves to danger. My daughter did not have "bad habits," like the police say. That's why I continue to say that my daughter did not leave; they took her. (H. Enriquez, personal communication, January 4, 2005)

Another Mother explains how the authorities articulated her daughter's "double life" as a gang member, drug addict, and prostitute, and forced her to look in the "zona rosa" [red-light/brothel district] for her:

I am Guadalupe Zavala, Mother of Érika Ivonne Ruiz Zavala. She disappeared the 23 of June, of 2001. Her body appeared semi-buried at the foot of a tomb of the graveyard that is near our home. The authorities concluded that it was not a homicide. They said that my daughter was a gang member—that she was in the neighborhood gangs—which is like a mark on her. The authorities investigate when they think the disappeared are good girls. They [authorities] have a scale of discrimination: the integrated, the studious, the rich—at the other end are the gang members and prostitutes. They told me to look for her in "la zona rosa"—that's why they never looked for her. And when she died, they

---

3. We went undercover, accompanied by activists, to a bar in the center of Juárez to see the hidden room where forced prostitution occurs. We observed a cutout in the ceiling, which is the hidden entry point. We learned that there are many of these "underground" locations throughout the city's bars.

blamed her. They said that she had died of an overdose—but they have never wanted to exhume the body so that they can take the proper tests, to be sure that she ingested substances—and that that was the cause of her stated death. (G. Zavala, personal communication, January 4, 2005)

Corruption / Government Involvement

Many of the Mothers, to this day, function as "truth tellers"—publicly denouncing the government's involvement in their daughters' disappearances and deaths. As Hesford and Kozol (2005) state, truth-telling discourses are "cultural narratives that articulate historical processes of oppression, resistance, and collective action" (p. 9). Through their rhetoric, the Mothers have functioned as fierce truth tellers—exposing the government corruption and collusion with the cartels surrounding the feminicidios:

What's going on? Are they . . . you . . . receiving a lot of money from someone powerful? Are they helping cover up these crimes? I really believe that they had something to do with the disappearances. (E. Arce, personal communication, June 27, 2016)

Patricia, Mother of Neyra, explains the corruption and cover-up in her daughter's case:

There is no way, after 55 days, that Neyra's body could be a pile of bones. It was already in the sixth stage of decomposition. The body must have been moved. They [the government] blamed Davíd [Meza]. They said that he walked up a mountain with her body in 45 minutes, at 7:00 p.m. at night. This mountain, "Cuernos de la Luna" [Horns of the Moon], is on the [property of the] police firing range, and the state police headquarters is on the other side—and we continue to see more deaths in Chihuahua. The authorities must be guilty, otherwise they would do something. (P. Cervantes, personal communication, October 25, 2004)

Veronica, a longtime labor organizer and feminicidio activist, relayed:

FIGURE 1.1. Government shooting range. Evidence about where Neyra and numerous other bodies were found is located on the state police shooting-range headquarters. This image I took also embodies the notion of women being killed "for sport" by high-ranking officials. Photo taken by author, Chihuahua, 2005.

The assassinations have to be by someone powerful . . . someone with a lot of money—who can't be blamed easily. The police haven't done anything to look for them. No information gets out. They don't really catch anybody. They can't find who did it, supposedly. The police are very well organized. When something is happening, they look the other way. They only act when there is more pressure put on them. (V. Lleva, personal communication, January 5, 2005)

Another family member of one of the disappeared extends Veronica's analysis:

They are the ones who disappear the people—and the evidence, because they have the capacity to do so. There are some who say that the archives are torn up, so it is someone with a lot of power. They are able to make phone records and evidence disappear. So, there are many things that we can't prove, but we know. (Anonymous, personal communication, June 25, 2016)[4]

Torture/Scapegoating

During the second wave of the feminicidios, as Ortiz (2016) has pointed out, many individuals were either tortured into confessing or scapegoated for the disappearances and murders so that the government could present the image to the world that justice was being served.[5] One of the most egregious cases of both torture and scapegoating is that of Patricia Cervantes's murdered daughter, Neyra, and her nephew, Davíd Meza. Davíd, Neyra's cousin, was tortured and scapegoated as the one responsible for her death, resulting in his three years of false imprisonment in the Chihuahua state prison. Patricia recounts how her nephew was tortured:

They forced Davíd to confess that he had accomplices that he had called from Chiapas—that they had kidnapped Neyra—and he had somehow facilitated a gun and money for them to use—and that then he returned to kill her . . . they forced him under torture to confess. They used electrodes on his testicles and poured chili powder in his eyes, nostrils and his mouth.[6] (P. Cervantes, personal communication, October 25, 2004)

---

4. For a complete accounting of the evidence of government involvement in the disappearances, see works by the investigative journalist Diana Washington Valdez listed in the bibliography.

5. For example, two of the most infamous cases, in addition to Davíd Meza's, include the government's scapegoating of Abdel Latif Sharif Sharif [The Egyptian] and members of Los Rebeldes [The Rebels] for multiple murders. Sharif died while incarcerated, and most of the "rebels" were released.

6. In addition to collecting Patricia's testimony about the torture, I visited Davíd in the Chihuahua state prison, where he was incarcerated while awaiting trial. Davíd described, in excruciating detail, the torture he experienced. After returning to Los Angeles, and after leading an alternative break trip to investigate the feminicidios, I and my students, at Loyola Marymount University, started a social justice group, Justicia Para Davíd Meza [Justice for Davíd Meza], to struggle for Davíd's freedom. Every Friday afternoon, for 18 months, students, activists, some of Davíd's family members, and I protested, in shifts, outside the Los Angeles Mexican Consulate to demand Davíd's

Davíd Meza's case of torture is not unique. And although there was ample physical evidence of torture, the judge, as referenced by his public remarks here, refused to admit the evidence of torture during Davíd's sentencing:

> You ask me, but wasn't there torture? But here I sit as the judge who denied the protective trial . . . that ruled that there was no demonstration of torture. I think that we must discover the point—or exact evidence of the torture. As a judge, unfortunately, you see confessions against the court. Confessions by torture—physically? No. Morally . . . threatened . . . intimidated . . . perhaps. (J. Rodriguez, personal communication, November 4, 2004)

Unfortunately, tortures and forced confessions in Mexico surrounding the feminicidios continue.

Movement Gains

Although, as demonstrated, the Mothers and activists experienced severe suppression strategies exerted by the Mexican government, during the second wave of the feminicidios, they were successful in exerting agency for systemic change to address these crimes. Because of the efficacy of the activists' strategies during this wave, the Mexican government, as well as international human rights bodies, not only were compelled to symbolically recognize the feminicidios as a real phenomenon but also were forced to enact structural material changes. Ortiz explains:

> In this period are the first steps to professionalize the government bodies in charge of the searches for the disappeared women. During this time, a special prosecutor to investigate the crimes was initiated, as well as the formation of government special institutes, etc. The phenomenon of feminicidio had become global, as exhibited in the International Caravan for Justice and International Court trials. The subject of feminicidio had now come to all corners of the world—such as the

release. Fortunately, after over two years in prison, Davíd was eventually released. To this date, no one has been held accountable for Neyra's murder.

European Parliament, and the Inter-American Court of Human Rights' historic judgment—the condemnation of the Mexican State as culpable of feminicidio—and being told that they must repair the damage to the victims of violence. While the "Cotton Field" decision was a triumph in terms of the sentence to a state, the truth was . . . that it was a partial repair—only a "solution" to a tiny part of the problem. The government now was like, "sorry," and "I forgot." It was obvious that real change was rejected and that the Mothers and civil society organizations had to continue with the fight because, in addition, women were still disappearing and being killed.

Inter-American Court of Human Rights Ruling

On November 6, 2001, eight bodies with evidence of extreme sexual violence were discovered in the Campo Algodonero [the Cotton Field]. As a result of the activism and international pressure exerted by the Mothers, three cases—Claudia Ivette González, Esmeralda Herrera Montreal, and Laura Berenice Ramos Monárrez—were brought before the Inter-American Commission on March 6, 2002, and presented to the International Court of Human Rights on November 16, 2009. Human rights attorney and longtime Chihuahua feminicidio activist Lucha Castro details her legal work on several of the killings:

In December 2003 we presented two cases before the Inter-American Commission: the case of Paloma Escobar, a young woman killed in Chihuahua City, and Silvia Arce, who disappeared in Juárez. And twice we have presented at the Commission for Human Rights, as a part of the United Nations, in Geneva, Switzerland. We also participated in a delegation that gave testimony before the High Commissioner of Human Rights before the United Nations. (Personal communication, November 2, 2004)

The historic judgment ruled that the killings constituted an infringement of the victims' rights to life, integrity, and personal freedom. In addition, the ruling found that the Mexican government had violated the rights of the victims' families to access to justice and judicial protection (*González et al. "Cotton Field" vs. Mexico*, 2009). By failing to prevent the disappearances and feminicidios of women, and to properly investigate cases in Ciudad Juárez, the ruling mandated, the state must conduct "serious murder investigations, and investigate law enforcement officials responsible for obstructing cases, fabricating evidence, and scapegoating and torturing victims" (Edley & Lozano-Reich, 2011, p. 131). Mexico was also mandated to, within one year of the ruling, build a monument as a memorial to the murdered women, hold a press conference and issue a public apology, publish criminal sentences in official government documents and newspapers, expand gender sensitivity and human rights training for police, step up and coordinate the efforts to locate the disappeared, permanently publicize the cases on the Internet, and properly investigate any reported harassment and death threats reported by victims' family members (*González et al. "Cotton Field" vs. Mexico,* 2009).[7]

The Cotton Field ruling holds four important consequences for setting a precedent against global forms of feminicidio against women, especially in Latin America: (1) the state has a responsibility to ensure human rights, (2) violence against women constitutes a form of gender discrimination, (3) monies must translate into structural protections, and (4) protocols for investigations must be regulated and adhered to (López, 2012). In addition, while Article 68 of the American Convention on Human Rights states that "the States Parties to the Convention undertake to comply with the judgement of the Court in any case to which they are parties," and, as the last line in the "Cotton Field" ruling states, "the Court will continue to monitor the State's compliance in its remaining obligations," in reality, the International Court has very little leverage to actually hold states accountable (López, 2012).

Argentinian Forensics Team

A monumental gain for the family members of the feminicidio victims was Mexico's agreeing to bring the Argentinian Forensic Anthropology Team [EAAF] into the state of Chihuahua to help identify the DNA of the feminicidio victims. This world-renowned forensic team previously

7. Although the ruling was historic, as one of the Mothers stated, "I don't want a monument; I want justice" (anonymous, personal communication, June 25, 2016). In addition, when the monument ceremony occurred, numerous Mothers boycotted the ceremony to demonstrate to the world that nothing had changed.

worked to identify victims of Argentina's "dirty war" and the Salvador-
ian civil war, and it helped identify victims of the September 11, 2001,
collapse of the World Trade Center Twin Towers (Roig-Franzia, 2007).
One Mother articulates the significance of having EAAF brought in to
identify their daughters' DNA samples:

> If it weren't for the Argentinean anthropologists, I would still be look-
> ing for my live daughter, because the authorities never told me that
> they found a woman's body in this place—even when there had been
> a disappearance report. (Anonymous, personal communication, Janu-
> ary 4, 2005)

Another activist shares:

> Four months later the police found the bones [of Maria Elena], but the
> first and second DNA tests came back negative. It wasn't until the third
> test that it was positive, so it was weird—so she [Julia, Mother of Maria
> Elena] may not trust the results. And that's very common—that the
> DNA matches, then it doesn't match, then it does. (L. Rocha, personal
> communication, June 20, 2016)

Thus, while EAAF has given the Mothers tremendous hope that
their daughters' remains will, indeed, be properly identified and
returned to them, the cases move extremely slow, and, unlike Europe
and the United States, Mexico has a statute of limitations of 14 years.

Changes in the Legal System

Successful pressure by the activists and family members also resulted
in key legal shifts during this wave. After the Mothers' 2003 caravan
to Mexico City, where they protested against then president Vicente
Fox, Fox allocated funds to create an official office to address the feminicidios. In 2004 the "Commission for the Prevention and Eradication of Violence Against Women in Ciudad Juárez" was opened. The
office was headed by Commissioner Guadalupe Morfín Otero. The
charge of her office was to, as stated, "prevent and eradicate violence."
Morfín's office purported to hold meetings with Mothers of victims,
publish data regarding the statistics on gendered crimes, offer psycho-

logical counseling, hold gender-sensitivity training, and collaborate on seminars regarding feminicidios with el Colegio de la Frontera Norte (COLEF). Again, while the implementation of a state-funded office to address gendered violence was viewed internationally as a large movement gain, one must ask whether the implementation had any significant effect on the decrease in gender violence.

For example, when our delegation met with Guadalupe Morfín and asked her what she had been doing to stop the feminicidios, she remarked that her office was "looking into putting lavender candles into the prisons, as well as building more soccer fields in the central zones." When I pressed her to explain what lavender candles and soccer fields do to solve feminicidio, she replied, "Lavender is shown to be soothing and calming—also, if men are using their testosterone on the soccer field, they will be less likely to be agitated." We walked out of the meeting.[8] Also of significant concern was that many women in Juárez, during this wave, had not heard of the "Alba Protocol," although it was Morfín's office that was responsible for this task.[9]

Karla Castañeda, Mother of Cinthia, one of the disappeared, recounts:

> She [government official] asked if they had carried out the Protocol Alba when my daughter went missing. I told her "I don't know what that is!" She explained that the Protocol Alba forces the authorities to look in the main areas of the city for a potentially missing person, regardless of how long she has been missing. I told her I didn't do that because I didn't know that it existed. (Personal communication, April 18, 2016)

Finally, in what has been described as "a revolution in Mexican justice," due to the movement's relentless calls for judicial change, the state of Chihuahua reformed its justice system to mimic US trials and to include open courtrooms and oral testimony (Ellingwood, 2009). Blanco (2009) demonstrates that this change has resulted in the increased reporting of crimes in the Mexican state of Chihuahua and an increase in the investigations undertaken by the fiscalía [prosecution office].

---

8. When President Vicente Fox left office, Morfín's office was shut down.
9. Mexico's "Alba Protocol" was modeled after the US's "Amber Alert."

WAVE THREE: 2010-2014

I refer to the third wave of violence in Ciudad Juárez as the lost years. During this time, Juárez saw the beginning of the militarization of the state. Due to the "narco wars," the Mothers' and activists' gains, as just laid out, had now completely stalled. Moreover, the state, during this third wave, silenced, banished, and purged feminicidio activists under the guise of the "narco wars." Originally advanced by Mbembe (2003), necropolitics refers to "the material destruction of human bodies and populations" (p. 14). Mbembe (2003) contends that states create "death worlds" through their targeted and strategic murder of people who are no longer useful to the state—or who do not fall in line with state practices and ideologies. Necropolitics, then, as a critical analytic framework addresses the ways that states and their institutions "dictate who may live and who must die" (Achille, 2003, p. 11).

Ortiz's (2016) analysis provides a comprehensive understanding of the societal conditions during this wave of the narco wars that functioned as a form of necropolitics of the state:

This period is characterized by the decline, disappearance or replacement of the objectives that some of the pioneering social organizations in the fight for justice had achieved. During this time period, the phenomenon of feminicidio is completely overshadowed—and sometimes completely invisible, due to the so-called war on drugs, decreed by President Felipe Calderón. The City went into a spiral of violence that led up to a peak of 3,500 murders per year—the majority of them in a savage manner. This meant that the feminicidio work went "flat." The main characteristic of this period was that the subject of feminicidio, and the "war on drugs," intersected.[10] As a result, some of the main leaders of the feminicidio movement, during the first wave, suffered constant threats of death for themselves and their families. This led to the emergence of a new social phenomenon: forced exile to the United States. Also at this stage, the state-sponsored murder of feminicidio activist Marisela Escobedo, Mother of feminicidio victim Ruby, and other prominent feminicidio activists occurred. Forced exile did not

---

10. Although the drug trade has always played an implicit role in the feminicidios, the narco wars peaked during this period.

only occur for the leaders of the feminicidio movement, but others who were defending human rights—activists and journalists were also affected. For instance, first-wave feminicidio activists such as Norma Andrade and Karla Castañeda were forced to flee Mexico for fear of execution. These exiles were the "excesses" of the federal forces stationed in Juárez during this time, in what was widely referred to as Calderón's War. The Reyes family, who were fighting against militarization, also fled. Journalists who were forced to flee included Rosa Isola Perez, Jorge Luis Aguirre, Ricardo Chavez—among others. The countries which have received Chihuahuenses as exiles from threats and risk include the United States, Canada, and Spain. Thus far, this phenomenon, the exile of Chihuahuenses, has not been studied.

As Ortiz (2016) explained, during these years, the feminicidios now became inherently linked to the militarization of the state. What is important to understand is that the government and the cartels are, in fact, one and the same entity:

> The other complicated problem in all of this is the narco-trafficking. It's widely believed that narco-traffickers and the very corrupt Chihuahua State police, which are heavily involved in trafficking are, in fact, the same entity—and are involved in some of these murders. There were reports for many years about rapes and murders on the part of police officers, but we got our very first concrete link earlier this year [2016]. In March [2016] there were 15 Chihuahua State officers who were a part of the group called la Línea [The Line], who were arrested when an informant led the authorities to 13 bodies buried under the home of one of these police officers. All of these bodies, men and women, were executed in a typical narco-trafficking style. However, the informant testified that this group of police officers was also involved in feminicidio. He said that when police officers would successfully traffic drugs into the US, one of the ways they would celebrate was by kidnapping, raping, and torturing a woman.

The militarization of the state crippled the strong public sphere through the reign of terror that ensued. Professor Julián Contreras of Ciudad Juárez (2016) explains this phenomenon:

We knew, of course, that there were many feminicidios, and from time to time executions in the style of narco-traffickers near the border. But before this time frame, there weren't any decapitations, or crucifixions or hangings—so these things hadn't been seen before. Some people took it as a joke, but then the executions and beheadings started happening regularly. These violent acts against the general population generated a feeling of discontent and very strong insecurity. From November 2007 to February 2008, the insecurity of general well-being was impressive. Because of this, we lived through a coordinated effort by the federal, state, and local governments to militarize the city and instill fear in the people. The military took to the streets to employ a campaign to try to win the people over, and to have the people believe that they were here to solve the problem—things like ceremonies— where a little girl gives flowers to the military men. This campaign allowed the state to be militarized in the beginning of March 2008. But if we see the number of executions from that first month we saw an increase of 400 percent—four times as many executions with the presence of the military! Because of this escalation of executions and massacres, the years 2008–2009 were really grave years. We [Juárez] went from executions of 3 to 4 people to massacres. There were also more disappearances and rapes of women. We understood that those [government and multinational corporations] established powers were the ones encouraging and benefiting from a supposed war against narcotrafficking. So, to us, it was an absurd notion that they were fighting against themselves. We knew they weren't here to combat these crimes . . . we didn't have a credible explanation as to how these commandos and militaries were walking around in full gear still executing people if all the city was pretty much militarized! When the massacres occurred here, there were militaries nearby, so when we saw that, we asked: how is this all possible if the city was occupied? But, again, this politics of war enabled women to be afraid and not want to push forward in public spaces. In these years, the killings of women hadn't ceased. There are still many disappearances, but not much activism. (Personal communication, June 20, 2016)

As investigative journalist Diana Washington Valdez explains, the terror felt by the masses, that Contreras communicated, resulted in an effective silencing of feminicidio activism:

Okay. The cartel wars interrupted the [feminicidio] activism. They interrupted the ability of people outside of Juárez, whether it's from other parts of Mexico or other countries, to enter that territory and do their investigations—yes, and journalists and academics and others. The only organization that I know that was able to go in at the request of the government was the Argentinian group. The other thing that happened in the cartel wars is that it became open season on the activists. The violence associated with them [cartel wars] provided the perfect cover to take out people that were inconvenient for the government. It's true. So that kind of has many repercussions. One of them was, of course, to silence people because others moved away from the area. I think it's sort of created a pause in the activism. The kind of activism that had been building up until then—the organized groundswell. People just started to back off. That was what the effect of the violence involving the drug cartels had on the feminicidio movement. (Personal communication, June 19, 2016)

Julián Contreras (2016) also explains how the militarization years were not only a gendered-based war on women but also a class-based war on the poor:

More than 90 percent of small businesses closed but we never saw Wal-Mart being attacked—or a Home Depot. None of the great businesses or great cathedrals/institutions were harmed. We were at "war," but somehow only the poor suffered. None of the big businesses were damaged. What we saw was that the war against narco-trafficking was targeted at the low-end crimes like petty theft, but the great heads of organized crime were never touched. So, from these examples, we knew that the war was against the poor . . . there were 120,000 homes—entire towns abandoned, for example, because people could no longer pay to keep them. This very space was one of those houses [*points across the street*]. It was just a shell, and we were able to fix it. So, for the people, it was a moment that true hunger was felt . . . what we saw was a repression of poor people. (Personal communication, June 20, 2016)

This third wave also saw scores of brutal assassinations of feminicidio, labor, and human rights activists. Contreras (2016) explains how the state used the "narco wars" as a pretext for the purging of activists:

FIGURE 1.2. Deserted colónia of Guadalupe. In January 2010 Josefina Reyes was gunned down and executed here. Following her assassination, three of her family members were also assassinated. They were all killed because of their ongoing activism against the state's militarization and human rights abuses. Photo taken by author, Ciudad Juárez, 2016.

All these exterminations could be carried out because the government was at war. So in Juárez, we were able to see another theme, which was the killing of social activists or anyone who was perceived as a threat to the system. Jimenez Ochoa organized against the militarization of the government, and he was executed the next day. Miguel Arroyo Galvan, a professor from the university researching the worker movement, was executed. Josefina Reyes, a pioneer against the militarization and feminicidios in the Valley of Juárez, was executed. Journalists and labor leaders were executed. So these executions carried less weight because people would think "it's just another narco death." An execution of a social activist in a time of peace, versus a time of war, is very different. (Personal communication, June 20, 2016)

Lluvia continues:

They started killing people, threatening them, raping women. Pretty much war. What we understand a war to be. So the official rhetoric was

"It's the organized crime doing it! It's the organized crime! It's the orga- nized crime!" but we know it wasn't organized crime. It was the state— the system, yes. (L. Rocho, personal communication, June 20, 2016)

Consequently, the feminicidios that occurred during these years, due to the "narco wars," were rendered invisible. In addition, the dev- astation of the working class, during the same period, also functioned to spotlight the intersectionality of gender and class:

In the case of the feminicidios, in 2008, there were only a few disap- pearances that got attention. There were a few Mothers that protested their daughter's disappearances who were from this period. The deaths of these women, however, were made invisible because of all the other deaths happening. There was no focus on why or how these women were killed in relation to men. I am almost certain that how the women were killed would lead us to the realization that the war that Calderon brought was part feminicidio. So, it's like saying, "I am not only kill- ing you because you are poor, but I am killing you because you are a poor working woman." (J. Contreras, personal communication, June 20, 2016)

Toward the end of this wave, a shift in consciousness among the feminicidio activists also began to emerge. Contreras expounds on this key point:

We must also battle certain legal points because some laws allow this impunity to go on. So how can we call this country a democracy when we have more than a quarter of a million people executed? This is the sort of context feminicidio happens in. The fight women carry out is largely against those who killed them, but it should be fighting against the system that allows this. The state allows for women to be killed because they allow for a misogynistic rhetoric to continue. This is what influences young men in this country, because the state allows mass media to provide this message. But I see that this realization is hap- pening with the activists. The politics of women is to denounce sexual abuse and aggression, which are unjustifiable, but we must also con- template that society is sick because the state encourages society to be this way. So, we must realize that feminicidio is a state crime—not only the murders by *an* individual. We must also look at the factors that allow this to happen. (Personal communication, June 20, 2016; emphasis added)

This ideological shift that emerged during these "lost years," as we will see, now critically frames the current strategies and tactics enacted in today's fourth-wave struggles for justice.

WAVE FOUR: 2015–PRESENT: MOVEMENT AND FEMINICIDIO RESURGENCES

Government Denial

To this day the Mexican government denies that the feminicidios ever occurred or currently exist. On February 19, 2015, during a press conference, then mayor of Ciudad Juárez Enrique Serrano Escobar continued to refer to the Juárez feminicidios as a "dark myth—a legend." Karla, Mother of Cinthia, expresses outrage that after decades of struggle, there is still feminicidio denial:

Dark legend? What the hell?! They are our daughters! They were kidnapped in Juárez! How can they say it was a legend if it keeps on happening? That's not a legend. These are real stories—my story, my friends' stories! Our daughters are not these dark legends! They are our daughters! And they were kidnapped in Juarez! (K. Castañeda, personal communication, April 8, 2016)

In June 2016, one month before my return to Juárez, eight women's corpses in one week alone were found discarded in a river canal near the El Paso border. The year 2016 logged 118 feminicidios, and, at the time of this writing, in 2017, seven feminicidios have already been documented.[11] Thus, while the material reality of the feminicidios in Juárez continues, this reality is often rendered invisible to wider publics because of the Mexican government's mythologizing of these killings. As Barthes (1972) reminds us, myths function as "depoliticized speech";

---

11. Note that this number is always fluid, and that statistics will differ depending on whom is asked. I cite my statistics from Professor Julia Monárrez-Fragoso, who is considered the most reliable source for Juárez feminicidio data.

therefore, if the Mexican government's myth prevails, political intervention and structural change are thwarted. Thus, family members and activists continue to engage in counterhegemonic strategies and tactics to counter this oppressive discourse. It is these projects that we turn our attention to now.

Resurgence of Feminicidio Activism

In 2015 we saw a resurgence of activism against the feminicidios. Although the Mexican government attempted to co-opt this fourth-wave emergent movement with its "Todos Somos Juárez" [We Are All Juárez] campaign, which consisted of pink ribbons and bumper stickers distributed by the Mexican government, a new generation of activists, who lived through the brutal repression of the lost years, mentored by activists from the first wave, saw through this tactic of attempted co-optation by the state.

Consequently, today, this fourth wave consists of a new generation of activists—or, as many young activists in Juárez define themselves, "the daughters of feminicidio." As Jessica states, "we have seen feminicidio firsthand. Our Mothers were survivors, and we are the daughters of the survivors." This current generation of frontline activist groups includes Rosas Rojas de Juárez [Red Roses of Juárez], Frenté Marginal [Marginal Front], Pink Nopál [Pink Cactus], Red Mesa de Mujeres [Board Network of Women], and Grupo de Acción por los Derechos Hermanos y la Justicia Social [Action Group for Human Rights and Social Justice], among others.

There are several key tenets of this fourth wave of antifeminicidio activism. First is the availability of social media to aid the groups' circulation of their messages into the wider public sphere. Thanks to social media, the fourth-wave activists are able to communicate and collaborate with the exiled activists, thus providing a communicative bridge across this physical gap. In addition to social media, I contend, the most significant gain in this fourth wave is the more visible involvement of men in the movement for justice. Three key men in the current movement against feminicidio are the activist and educator Señor Don José Luis Castillo, Father of Esmeralda Castillo Rincón,[12]

---

12. Esmeralda disappeared when she was 14 years old. Her Father has been searching for her ever since.

the professor and activist Julián Contreras, and the graffiti and rap artist Maclovio, who are members of Frenté Marginal [Marginal Front]. The activist work of these men is highlighted, along with that of the other aforementioned activist groups, in chapters 2 through 5. These groups, building upon the generational work of the early Mothers groups and aforementioned NGOs, are now leading the movement against the feminicidios. Finally, as referenced in Contreras's testimony, this fourth wave's rhetorical strategies not only function to indict an *individual* perpetrator of a feminicidio, but rather turn its strategic sensibilities towards indicting the material *systems* that give rise to feminicidio in the first place. As we are currently in the midst of the fourth wave of violence, as I write this text, I hope that future studies continue to extend this archive as antifeminicidio movements continue—because, unfortunately, it is unlikely that the killing of women and girls will cease under the curent sociopolitical and economic conditions.

CHAPTER 2

Feminicidio and the "Enchanted" Assemblages of Things

THIS CHAPTER troubles the new materialist posthumanistic turn wherein human agency and motive are replaced across a spectrum of "assemblages." In Bennett's (2005) advocating for a turn toward an underdetermined starting point where "nonhuman materialities [function] as actors" (p. 466), agency is simultaneously dispersed across all contexts so that it is hence everywhere and thus nowhere. Bennett's (2005) "distributive theory of agency" argues that "effective agency is always assemblage: it is constituted by the interplay of human and non-human materialities" (p. 454). Extending Bennett's (2005) work, Pflugfelder (2015) contends that we must conceive of agency as "attuned to . . . material conditions" (p. 442). Indeed, historical materialism has always adhered to this proposition. Where historical materialists and new materialists depart is in the premise that all human and nonhuman assemblages are afforded the *same* agency and effects. As this chapter will demonstrate, when new materialists view the weight of agency dispersed equally across assemblages, we are left with a blunted agency—one where historical forces are muted and human and nonhuman "intra-activity" is granted equal societal significance. Consequently, because of the silence of theories of new materialism on the relationship between things and neoliberalism, new materialism is effectively complicit with its oppressive structures and thereby power-less to combat its devastating effects.

It is only fitting to challenge new materialists' articulation of human and nonhuman "intra-activity" (Barad, 2007, p. 152) through the assemblages of things by examining the site where things themselves are indeed assembled: the maquiladoras. New materialists contend that the relationship between human and nonhuman elements should be viewed in ways that are "insufficiently fixed and predictable" (Bennett, 2015, p. 85). However, as Washick and Wingrove (2015) point out, "for the historically situated, decidedly nonmetaphysical 'masters' and 'slaves' of global capitalism, such giddy underdetermination concerning subject positions might get in the way" (p. 66). Indeed, new materialism's inability to account for neoliberal forces can best be found in Bennett's (2010) naïve embrace of "enchanted materialism." Bennett (2010) locates the enchantment of materialism in the assemblages of things:

> For had the sun not glinted on the black glove, I might not have seen the rat; had the rat not been there, I might not have noted the bottle cap, and so on. But they *were* [emphasis in original] all there just as they were, and so I caught a glimpse of an *energetic vitality* [emphasis added] inside each of these things. (p. 5)

Bennett's ability to find these things "enchanting," I contend, is because the assemblage of these things is divorced from a context and history of said things. For example, if we take Bennett's examples and contextualize them within the free-trade zone of Ciudad Juárez, would the Juárenses be as enchanted? In Juárez, for example, gloves needed to stay warm are often in short supply, bottle caps are often scavenged to exchange for money as a means of economic sustenance, and rats, dead or otherwise, are in no shortage in the colónias, where many workers live in extreme poverty due to the lack of state public infrastructure, such as proper sanitation.

In the murder capital of the world, there is no enchantment; instead, the assemblage of things is most often *assembled,* through the women of Juárez's labor, on an assembly line, in an 18-hour day, as a means of survival. The assemblage of things is not "insufficiently fixed and predictable" (Bennett, 2015, p. 85) but instead is determined by neoliberal free-trade agreements, resulting in exploitation, suffering, and feminicidio, a far cry from new materialists' privileged centering of the trope of enchantment. The assemblage of things explored in this chapter includes mechanical parts, machinery, pregnancy sticks, feminine pads, roads, buses, sidewalks, lights, and sanitation. To align myself with critics of new materialism, such as Edwards (2010), who suggests that when interrogating the assemblages of things scholars must "return to a kind of historical materialism that focuses on the reproduction of capitalist societies and the system of states, both in everyday practices of production and consumption and in the ideological and coercive power of states and the international system" (p. 283), we must first look at the history of Ciudad Juárez and its relationship to neoliberalism, in order to understand the correlation between the assemblage of things and feminicidio.[1]

BRACERO PROGRAM

Ciudad Juárez is the largest city in the Mexican state of Chihuahua. It is currently populated by roughly 1.5 million "Juárenses." Juárez borders the US states of Texas and New Mexico, with most of Juárez nestled against El Paso:

> The City of Juárez was an indigenous Manzo territory. When the conquerors crossed these lands, they named it Paso del Norte [the way North], for being a strategic location. Today we know it as Camino Real. This land was known as a place to stop and rest on the way to

---

1. The past and current history of Ciudad Juárez, laid out in this chapter, is informed by two personal interviews that I conducted with two university professors in Juárez and with a member of Mexico Solidarity Network's Steering Committee. Dr. Felix L. Pérez Verdugo is a professor of history at the Universidad Pedagógica Nacional del Estado de Chihuahua de Ciudad Juárez [the National University of Pedagogy in the State of Chihuahua in Ciudad Juárez]. Professor Julián Contreras Alvarez is a professor of literature at the Universidad Autonoma de Ciudad Juárez [Autonomous University of the City of Juárez]. Felix and Julián are also longtime activists and native Juárenses. Julián is a founding member of the activist group Frenté Marginal [Marginal Front]. Jessica Marquez worked on the ground with the Mothers in Juárez during the period of 2002–2007 and led numerous campaigns and speaking tours educating publics about the relationship between NAFTA and feminicidio.

New Mexico. It was a dry and deserted place, located really close to the Rio Bravo. In 1939, the Second World War began. From 1939 to 1945, this had terrible consequences for Mexico. The country was going through an economic crisis, and there was a lot of unemployment. The United States had run out of manpower [sic] because most of the men were being recruited as soldiers and had gone to fight the Second World War. A program between the United States and Mexico was created and titled Braceros; Mexican citizens were recruited to go work in the United States—in the fields, on the railroads, or in places where manpower [sic] was most needed. In 1961, in anticipation of the major crisis approaching, the National Border Program–ProNaf [National Front Program] was created. It was aimed to generate employment and bring tourism back into the country. This was done because of the many deportations experienced by the same Mexican citizens recruited to work in the US under the Braceros program. In 1965 ProNaf failed to succeed; it did not generate as many jobs as expected. They [Mexican government] disregarded important sectors, and that is when the Border Industrial Program—the maquiladoras—were implemented.[2] The very first maquiladora was built in 1966. By 1970 the population increased to 407,370 inhabitants, and there were 22 maquiladoras established in the city. These maquiladoras employed more than 3,000 people. Ten years later, in 1980, there were 60 maquiladoras that provided jobs for more than 37,171 people. From its origin, maquiladora workers were mostly made up of women, and the few men working there were leaders, managers, and supervisors. The fact that women made up the majority of the maquiladora workers meant that it was changing the sociocultural and economic life of the country. Suddenly, men were displaced in their family leadership roles as providers, and women began to experience greater economic independence. Also, many of the immigrants coming from the center or south of the country to cross to the US, or to work in the maquiladoras, fell into great despair. They either were unable to cross the border or did not find any

---

2. The maquiladoras have a very specific function pertaining to assembly-line work: "The maquiladora is a company where one part of product is generated. These companies have their subsidiaries in the US or some other country. In Mexico, we do the labor work and the other countries take care of the administrative aspect of the final product. These maquiladoras provide the assembly of parts in order to create a product to be sold elsewhere" (F. L. Pérez, personal communication, June 27, 2016).

monetary benefits in the maquiladora industry. This led to increased drug trafficking and various forms of corruption among police authorities. (F. L. Pérez, personal communication, June 27, 2016)

NAFTA

In addition to the failure of ProNaf, the current economic devastation in Ciudad Juárez was aided by the passage of the North American Free Trade Agreement (NAFTA). Due to the effects of global neoliberal free trade, Bowden (1998) argued that Juárez functions as "the laboratory of our future." As my research will demonstrate, Juárez is a failed neoliberal laboratory experiment with devastating consequences. To understand the neoliberal elements that produce feminicidio, one must examine the structural transformations that have occurred since NAFTA's inception in conjunction with the feminicidios in Juárez. As Mohanty (1997) reminds us, it is necessary to place the feminicidios within their socioeconomic context to address the relationship between the feminicidios and capitalist modes of production: "The manner by which capital utilizes particular spaces for differential production and the accumulation of capital . . . transforms these spaces and people" (p. 5).

It is no coincidence that the feminicidios, as a socioeconomic-political phenomenon, began to appear shortly after the passage of NAFTA. Moreover, I contend that the worth of women, in Ciudad Juárez, is inextricably linked to the labor conditions that the women occupy. Roughly 60 percent of young women in Juárez compose the maquiladora sector. Additionally, many of the feminicidio victims work in the maquiladoras. On average, female maquiladora workers earn roughly $3.00 to $6.00 per day. When a woman gets fired from her job in the maquiladora sector, there are thousands of other women able to easily substitute her role. Based on these structural reasons, the female workers in Juárez are materially readily disposable and easy to replace: "It's no big deal for the factories; they just replace one woman with another" (V. Leyva, personal communication, June 27, 2016). Therefore, as stated, although some scholars contend that the trope of the "disposable body" undermines justice movements' attempts to stop feminicidio by reifying the inevitability of violence on women's bodies (e.g., Schmidt Camacho, 2004; Molloy, as quoted in Hooks, 2014), I contend that a turn away from the question of what makes the women in Juárez easily "disposable" obfuscates attention to the material-discursive forces that give rise to feminicidio in the first place. As Wright (2006) explains:

> The disposable . . . woman's body is not the same as the one that women workers bring into the workplace. Rather, it is a body manufactured during the labor process via discourses that combine bits and pieces of workers' bodies with industrial processes and managerial expectations. (p. 45)

Moreover, as I will demonstrate, the neoliberal "assemblage of things" surrounding the female maquiladora worker within the Juárez free-trade zone has a direct correlation with the feminicidios and other forms of violence on women's bodies. As J. Marquez explains:

> First of all, these murders began to accelerate between 1993 and 1994, and that was around the time that NAFTA went into effect. NAFTA went into effect on January 1, 1994. We [Mexico Solidarity Network] don't believe that this is a coincidence. This was a time period when people were coming in droves to Ciudad Juárez. They were migrating from other parts of Mexico when they could not continue to maintain their way of life in their respective homes. (Personal communication, November 28, 2003)

MAQUILADORAS

Currently, there are approximately 330 maquiladoras in the free-trade zone of Ciudad Juárez, employing roughly 280,000 factory workers—nearly 30 percent of the city's total number of laborers. Maquiladora workers earn, typically, between 3 and 6 US dollars per day, or an average of 39 cents per hour for a 10-hour day (Semuels, 2016). Most of the plants are foreign-owned, with eight of the 17 largest maquiladoras belonging to US corporations. Workers assemble things for corporations such as Foxconn, Hewlett Packard, Cisco, Delphi, Lear, and Dell (Bacon, 2016). The "assemblage of things" includes parts ranging from laptops to cartridges for inkjet printers to cell phones to televisions to airplane and automobiles (Bacon, 2015). Women make up over half the labor force (F. Pérez, personal communication, June 27, 2016).

Because most families cannot afford childcare, which would cost roughly 220 pesos per week, female maquiladora workers are most often forced to work the graveyard shifts, which are often 12 hours (V. Leyva, personal communication, June 27, 2016). Additionally, because workers cannot afford to live near the maquiladoras, most women live in the colónias, on the outskirts of town, miles from the factories. A former Juárez labor organizer explains how these conditions emerged:

> Look at what happened with NAFTA. NAFTA brought a lot of jobs to the border communities here. Wow, great. Mexico now has another source of income. That is fantastic. But what is happening now—what was supposed to be a solution—is now a huge problem. Juárez had a tremendous influx of people. For example, when Fuji came over here and decided they wanted to hire 5,000 people, they had over 50,000 people applying for the job! They came from everywhere, and they brought their families with them. As you know, by going out to the outskirts, people can't even live in the city anymore because there is no housing. And if there is housing available, it is extremely expensive. So they [the workers] are going to the outskirts of Juárez, where workers often construct their homes from discarded materials from the maquiladoras. (M. Cardenas, personal communication, November 4, 2004)

So, while corporations have reaped the profits of Mexican cheap labor, as Marx and Engels (2005) postulated, "it has resolved personal worth into exchange value . . . [and] has set up that single, unconscionable freedom—Free Trade. In one word, for exploitation . . . it has substituted naked, shameless, direct, brutal exploitation" (p. 11).

The women travel to and from the maquiladoras by bus, often for a fee. However, because the colónias often do not contain paved roads, the buses regularly stop miles from the workers' homes. Working conditions inside the factories are also dangerous, yet workers have little recourse to fight for better working conditions because of the loop-

FIGURE 2.1. Dwellings in Lomas de Poleo. Although most of the residents labor at the maquiladoras, producing goods for multinational corporations, basic services like sanitation and electricity are unsecured. Pictured is one of the main roads where women must walk for miles, with no lighting or sidewalks, to and from the factory bus stops. Eight bodies were found here in 1996. Photo taken by author, Ciudad Juárez, 2016.

holes in NAFTA as well as the fact that the "unions" in Ciudad Juárez are controlled by the political partnerships between the multinational corporations and the Mexican government.[3]

---

3. Of note, in 2016 maquiladora workers from the Commscope factory organized a sit-in, for 45 days, after workers who held a meeting in an attempt to organize were fired. The goal of the public sit-in was to raise awareness about unfair working conditions and non-living wages. The workers' primary demands included gaining access to a nonpartisan union and getting their jobs reinstated. The workers held press conferences and worked with attorneys and human rights consultants to circulate their demands. At the end of the 45 days, although the workers obtained permission to unionize, the 173 who were fired from the Commscope factory had not been rehired. Additionally, the union instillation has not translated to fair labor practices as of this writing. It remains to be seen whether these labor actions spread to other maquiladoras.

US NEOLIBERAL CULPABILITY

As explained in the introduction, although the Inter-American Court of Human Rights found the country of Mexico culpable of feminicidio, the decision rendered failed to indict the role of the multinational corporations—most of them US-owned—in the ruling. Thus, I extend Bejarano's (2013) femicidal definition of "state-sponsored feminicidio" and contend that the feminicidios in Juárez should be demarcated as "state-corporate feminicidio." Roughly 80 percent of maquiladoras are US-owned. Most of the products assembled by the female maquiladora workers are consumed by US citizens. As Wise (2006) has argued, NAFTA and the Mexican workforce are a form of US transnational imperialism. US corporations' "solutions" to the lack of safety for female maquila workers, to date, is sorely inadequate:

> Several corporations' "solutions" to the disappearances and murders have been to provide the workers with bottles of pepper spray, whistles, and self-defense classes. One maquiladora had the idea of giving women walkie-talkies, but that never happened. There were also discussions about placing safety personnel on the buses, but that also never happened. But the majority [of corporations] have completely ignored the problem to this day. (V. Leyva, personal communication, June 27, 2016)

In addition to the corporations' culpability in the feminicidios due to the lack of infrastructure and safety mechanisms, all of the Mothers' public testimony, since 2003, expresses a strong belief that the corporations and their personnel, in collusion with the state, are *themselves* directly involved in the female workers' forced disappearances and murders. One Mother of a feminicidio victim details:

> Twenty-eight days after her disappearance, they found eight women's bodies in the "Campo Algodonero" [Cotton Field] in front of the building of the association of maquiladoras [AMAC], and they said one of those women was my daughter. They found all of the eight bodies in strange circumstances. The newspaper says they found a man who was walking towards his home when he stumbled upon the remains of one

of the bodies. However, they later stated that one of the women had been dead for six months and was killed in that place [the cotton field]. The maquila is surrounded by residences and offices. Also, the maquiladora association is right next to the field. They [corporations] also have security cameras everywhere. Many of the girls also report having the corporations take their pictures. I am convinced that they are connected to the women disappearing from the factories. So, how is it then, that in six months, no one had come across anything until that day[4]? Did they throw their bodies there recently? Where did they have them?[5] (J. González, personal communication, May 1, 2004)

A former maquiladora worker shared her experience of her neighbor's daughter being raped by her shift boss:

One of our neighbors made $30.00 per week. She was a 14-year-old girl. She accepted an invitation from her factory boss. On her way home from work, around 8:00 at night, she came home with her clothes torn on a dark street. She came walking up towards the house like a zombie. She had semen on her shirt, and was crying. Her boss had drugged and raped her. These are the kinds of curses that have progressed since the maquiladoras have come to Mexico. Worse are the feminicidios. (Anonymous, personal communication, January 6, 2006)

Another longtime activist and founding member of Nuestras Hijas de Regreso a Casa relates:

Within the analysis that our organization, Bring Our Daughters Home, has made in relation to the assassinations and the maquiladoras—we have found that it's possible that there are people who have infiltrated the maquiladoras and have helped the assassins of these women—to find them and capture them. We know that, for example, there were some women who were captured shortly after they changed shifts— shortly after they changed maquiladoras—when they arrived for

---

4. During my first delegation to Juárez, the Mothers always made it a point to visit this site to have us physically stand there to witness how close the maquiladora association is to the abandoned cotton field. There were cameras, as well, surrounding the AMAC building.

5. Josefina is the Mother of feminicidio victim Claudia Ivette González.

work—only a couple minutes late. This leads us to believe that there are people within the maquiladoras who are identifying these women for assassination. (M. Ortiz, personal communication, November 2, 2005)

DISPOSABLE BODIES

Maquiladora workers must be analyzed through the system they occupy. As Salzinger's (2003) work reminds us, due to global capitalism, the female transnational worker's worth is equated with cheap and docile feminized labor. As stated, in Juárez women earn very little, and they are constantly under threat of being fired, as there are thousands of other bodies ready to replace them. As pointed out in the preface, most of the feminicidio victims are migrants, poor, attractive, and young. Because many of the young female workers are forced to migrate north to find work, if a woman disappears from the assembly line, or on her way to or home from work, there is often no one to look for her (J. Marquez, personal communication, November 1, 2004).

Thus, the female maquiladora worker is easily disposable—or, as Wright (2001b) suggests, "waste in the making" (p. 561). Jessica Marquez explains Wright's (2001b) concept:

When people have come to Ciudad Juárez, it has been the women who have been able to find jobs in the maquiladoras. In addition, because women are coming by themselves, this has created a class of very easily preyed-upon poor, young women, which leads to a situation where women can be picked off very easily, and where men aren't afraid to do it. (Personal communication, November 1, 2004)

This analysis is supported by work from Livingston (2004): "The construction of working women as 'cheap labor' and disposable within the system makes it possible, and perhaps acceptable, to kill them [women and girls] with impunity" (p. 60). Another former maquiladora worker has witnessed this phenomenon firsthand:

They throw away any people who are unnecessary. That's what happened in my case . . . when we are not valued anymore, they just get rid

of us. In some cases, we're needed, in other cases we're disposable . . .
all they are interested in is production. Some of the women disappear
right off the line. (V. Leyva, personal communication, January 4, 2005)

In addition to the disposability of the female body inherently linked
to its capital worth, neoliberal economic forces collide with gendered
cultural discourses.

DISRUPTION OF GENDERED NORMS

Maquiladora managers prefer a female labor force. While plant managers report that women workers are better equipped for assembly-line
work because of their smaller hands and, hence, dexterity, it is well
documented that the corporations seek to hire women because they
can be paid less, they are more easily sexually harassed, and they can
be pressured to give sexual "favors." A former Juárez labor organizer
explains:

And we know that here in the border region, in particular Ciudad
Juárez, maquiladoras hire more young women, and this has been happening for a long time. The people who contract with these women
state that women are hard workers and do a better job. But, we know
from interviewing many women that, more than anything, they can
control them—harass them—and that they can pay them less. (M.
Cardenas, personal communication, January 3, 2005)

As a result of forced economic migration, and of the lack of means
of survival other than factory work, the gendered equilibrium of the
Mexican traditional family household was abruptly and significantly
disrupted. For example, although men were traditionally the breadwin-
ners, women were now forced to leave the home and find jobs in the
maquiladoras to feed their families. This neoliberal shift has created
a condition whereby men feel emasculated and disempowered. Felix
Pérez explains this dramatic cultural shift:

These factors triggered these conditions and generated a kind of
uncontrollable social disease in the city—because of the deficiencies

and forms of social pressure our citizens were facing. The feminiza-
tion of work meant that no longer were only men the ones behind
the production lines. Now there were women there—and the work
was "feminized." The fact that women were getting involved in labor
roles—in the production sector—drastically changed their social lives.
It changed the whole country's lifestyle. (F. Pérez, personal communication, June 27, 2016)

This "social disease," as Professor Pérez calls it, involved a violent
backlash against women—in both the private and public spheres. As
data collected by Casa Amiga has proved, domestic violence incidences
soared (L. Cordero, personal communication, July 28, 2016).[6] Marisela
Ortiz, one of the first-wave activists, provides analysis:

> The man who comes here looking to better his economic position finds
> that he cannot get a job, but rather his wife is hired. Then he has to take
> on work that, in a male-dominated "machismo" society, is not some-
> thing he is accustomed to taking on: cleaning the house, taking care
> of the children, cooking, et cetera. This creates a situation in which he
> then responds in a negative, "macho" way. So this generates confusion
> and animosity. It also generates a situation in which very often there
> is an outburst of violence—not just against the woman, but also the
> children. (Personal communication, November 2, 2005)

This violent backlash has also resulted in the killing of women. Former Juárez mayoral candidate and longtime activist Victoria Caraveo
explains:

> It's a crime because I hate you . . . that's why I kill you. Because I
> hate you. In Juárez, I think that we can't justify it, but we can under-
> stand. Because when it [the feminicidios] began, women here began
> to become more independent, because of the maquiladoras. Women
> began to work and have their own finances. And I think that that was
> very troubling for men to accept. It becomes violent rage. A common

---

6. Lydia Cordero is the director of Casa Amiga. For complete statistics on domestic violence incidents in Juárez, refer to their webpage: http://www.casa-amiga.org.mx.

saying now is, "if you don't behave you're going to end up in Lóte Bravo." (Personal communication, June 28, 2016)

Marx (1977), when writing about the effects of labor, describes the dehumanizing process as converting "the worker into a crippled monstrosity" (p. 481).

WORKERS AS PROSTITUTES

In Juárez, women who occupy public spaces, and especially the workforce, are coded as "prostituting themselves"—selling their bodies for corporate wages. A former maquiladora worker explains:

By working in the maquiladora, you were either labeled a lesbian or a whore, so you already enter the workforce with that guilt. My neighbors would not talk to me: "Oh no, she goes *out* to the maquiladoras at night; you can't talk to her." (V. Leyva, personal communication, January 4, 2005; emphasis in original)

As Anzaldúa's (2007) work reminds us, being viewed as a whore is a common oppressive narrative, whereby women must conform to the virgin/whore dichotomy. However, in the current neoliberal capitalist context, the ideology of the virgin is not inherently viewed as a protected or sacred identity. In the context of neoliberalism, the female virgin factory worker succumbs to the ideology of production:

They [male supervisors] are obsessed with the virgin. Groups of men huddle around women at the maquiladora: "Oh, she's mine." Girls in the maquiladoras have sex at 12, 13, and 14. The men can pinpoint who is a virgin. They only stay a virgin for two months, at the most. (V. Leyva, personal communication, January 4, 2005)

Thus, for the female factory worker, the virgin/whore dichotomy cannot be transcended—both subject positions lead to the inevitability of disposable capital—or, as Wright (1999) suggests, "death by culture" (p. 469).

INFRASTRUCTURE MATTERS

The feminicidios in Juárez are structural, not individual, crimes. State-corporate crimes are a result of the failure of the neoliberal economic model—or, to use Berndt's (2013) phrase, the "economization by maquiladorization" (p. 2648). Countless women have been beaten, raped, and murdered while going to and from the maquiladoras. It is my contention that women's bodies are vulnerable precisely because of their relationship to the objects and things both within and outside the maquiladora sector's free-trade zones.

Workers inside the maquiladoras are often at risk because of the objects they come into contact with. One maquiladora worker describes an injury she experienced while working at the Phillips Manufacturing maquiladora:

> I was working at a water bottle factory. The day the accident happened, I was stationed on a machine in charge of taking out the air so that the cap can go on the bottle. While I was making sure the bottles were sealed properly, there was an increase in pressure on the machine and the machine fell on me. It came down at the altitude of my eyes. Days later I went to get medical assistance and they told me there was a cornea detachment. They gave me severance pay, so that I could get help outside the public health system. It was not sufficient. A cornea costs 30,000 pesos. They only gave me 1,600 pesos. My vision is also not very good. I have many consequences, now, because of the accident. I get constant migraines, for example. I was told that I was getting help for the operation over two years ago, but nothing has happened. (Anonymous, personal communication, January 2, 2004)

In addition to posing risks to the workers who must interact with them, objects also function to control women's bodies. Women in the maquiladora sector, for example, are often forced to prove that they are menstruating by showing the managers their tampons and pads. Other female workers are forced to take pregnancy tests. One maquiladora worker shares her experience:

I want to also add an important matter: if the woman wanting to get hired is pregnant, then she is not hired. When you are requesting to get hired, a pregnancy test is performed. They also demand to check to see your pads each month in order to prove that you are bleeding. If you aren't, they will fire you sometimes. Last year I was pregnant. There is a lot of discrimination. You have to work as much as the others. You still only get two bathroom breaks, 10 minutes each. If you are not feeling well, you cannot ask permission to leave because you are expected to be there for eight hours. They discriminate a lot against pregnant women, because they think pregnant women are not capable of doing the things the other workers can. (Anonymous, personal communication, January 2, 2004)

Livingston's (2004) research supports this testimony: "Pregnancy tests are routinely administered. Mexican law requires social security coverage of pregnant women during the third trimester, and the maquiladoras would have to pay. Therefore, any woman who is pregnant is dismissed or harassed until she quits" (p. 62). As demonstrated, then, these objects function as sexual markers of hegemonic power. They are wielded by a woman's supervisor as a mechanism to regulate and dictate her ability to operate in a manner that is free of harassment and control.

In addition to experiencing the dangers of occupying the factory space, women are often the most vulnerable when they are walking to and from their work shifts, through the desert roads in the middle of the night, in the colónias of Anapra and Lomas del Poleo.[7] One former maquiladora worker explains these external dangers within the free-trade zone:

The maquiladoras view women as expendable and will fire women at any time. Many women are told that they are fired, and must leave on the spot. This leaves the women with no choice but to walk home alone before the buses come. For example, one woman, for no reason, was given a shift change so that she had to leave work without the protec-

---

7. One of the most infamous feminicidio cases involved the discovery of eight bodies of female maquiladora workers, found dumped on the side of a desert road at the top of Lomas del Poleo.

tion of her family. She disappeared that same afternoon, and her body was discovered 24 hours later. Another woman showed up four minutes late to work, and she was locked out. She never made it home. (Anonymous, personal communication, January 2, 2004)

Another former maquiladora worker also shared her experience:

We get out at two or three in the morning. I am always afraid, but we have to go out. There's also a lot of robbery of women at the maquiladoras. And at night, they let us out with no lights on. We have to wait until the bus comes. But many times the buses don't come, so we must walk home. The maquiladoras have done nothing about the feminicidios. (Anonymous, personal communication, January 4, 2005)

In addition to being the victims of rape and theft, female workers have been murdered while coming and going to and from their factory shifts. One father lost his daughter when she was forced to walk home alone, at night, through the desert, in the pitch black: "The bus should have dropped her off in front of the house, which never happened, and shortened the life of my daughter, whose only passion was school and her job. She wished to become a psychologist" (Hernandez, 2004). A Juárez labor activist describes another feminicidio victim who lost her life after the factory locked her out:

This happened at the Omega Industrial Park. Lear is the second largest maquiladora. One feminicidio victim worked here. Lear stated no responsibility after she was locked out and became a feminicidio victim. It happened on their property, yet they took no responsibility. She was not the first that this happened to. (T. Hansen, personal communication, January 5, 2005)

However, instead of investing in the safety and well-being of the factory workers, the maquiladoras, employing a neoliberal logic, instead invest their resources to expand their own capital:

If you look at the city, the best streets are connected to the maquiladoras. Governmental support is geared more for the benefit of foreign companies, which are transnational maquiladoras. There is little support for the domestic industry, and it is not their priority to develop support for health, education, and fieldwork. Their priority here is for industrial development. All the infrastructure for NAFTA transnational corporations is for the benefit of the maquiladora industry. The maquiladoras have everything they need—paved roads, lights, grass— and the workers continue to live in misery. (T. Hansen, personal communication, November 2, 2004)[8]

Workers, as Wright (2001a) echoes,

are the ones who must figure out a way to live in a city without enough housing, without enough water pipes or drainage systems, without electrical wiring that stretches to the new neighborhoods being built from whatever materials these migrant workers can find. (p. 109)

For example, as of this writing, in the colónias where most of the maquiladora workers live, there are numerous areas that contain

zero potable water, zero sewage, 5 percent paving, and 15 percent electricity. In all colónias, beyond the lack in basic services, there is severe abandonment in terms of social assistance, cultural centers, libraries and rehabilitation units to the over 200,000 workers who inhabit these neighborhoods. (Carrera, 2016)[9]

So, although union demands have included calls for higher wages, shorter workdays, and safer working conditions, the demands rarely exceed the geographic parameters beyond the boundaries of the factories themselves. However, it is *outside* the boundaries of the maquiladoras—the colónias where the workers live—that physical matter has a

8. Tom Hansen, PhD, is the past and current director of the NGO Mexico Solidarity Network. He is also the founder of the first critical social movement study-abroad programs in Latin America with sites in Mexico and Cuba: the Autonomous University of Social Movements (AUSM). He is a longtime community organizer. We traveled together during the Mothers' Caravan for Justice campaign, and he and I collaborated on my delegations with Loyola Marymount University students. For more information on this organization, or the study-abroad program, please visit http://www.mexicosolidarity.org/.

9. Benjamín Carrera is a professor of economics and agroindustries at the Autonomous University of Ciudad Juárez.

direct correlation to women's safety. Indeed, US owners of the maquiladoras know this. In 2013, for example, in recognition of the hazardous matter that the workers' bodies must navigate to and from work, the factory owners of the newly built "megamaquiladora" constructed a superhighway,[10] complete with paved roads and well-lit streets. The superhighway transports US factory managers directly from El Paso to the maquiladora plant, thereby effectively avoiding the hazardous worker labor route (Berndt, 2013).

As Marx conceived:

> Now, for the capitalist to undertake road building as a business, at his expense, various conditions are required, which all amount to this, that the mode of production based on capital is already developed to its highest stage . . . commercial, above all—that the road pays for itself, i.e., that the price demanded for the use of the road is worth that much exchange value for the producers, or supplies a productive force for which they can pay that much. (quoted in de la Haye, 1979, p. 42)

In addition to the insulated superhighway, the US factory managers now also live in a constructed "safe zone," as part of "a new industrial and residential hub along the border adjacent to the new San Agustín plant" (Berndt, 2013, p. 2652). As Welsome (2007) explains, this new plan benefits factory owners and corporations by creating a "savvy hybrid that . . . take[s] advantage of the rules—and lack of rules—in both countries" (p. 17). So, while women in Juárez who primarily live in Anapra and Lomas del Poleo will be left behind in what Berndt (2013) deems the third wave of maquiladorization, this geographical shift and displacement of women function simultaneously to demonstrate neoliberalism's success. As Wright (2004) explains, "the less and less we see of her [female factory worker], the more we recognize how far the maquiladora industry has come" (p. 374).

---

10. To gain access to build this superhighway, the high-powered Zaragoza family, in collusion with the state, terrorized Anapra residents with electric fences, barbed wire, and surveillance towers. People were harassed and routinely threatened. Luis Guerrero was beaten to death, and two young children were burned alive in a "mysterious" house fire. As of this writing, only eight families from the original 250 where the superhighway was built remain. The land is still under dispute for the larger territory of Anapra.

(RE)ASSEMBLAGES OF THINGS AS RESISTANCE

As the unions' attempts at maquiladora reforms have been effectively quelled by the Mexican government's control of the unions, some maquiladora workers have chosen to assemble *new* things to transform their relationship to capital. One such group, consisting solely of women, called Las Hormigas [The Ants], is located in the colónia of Anapra. This community of women, most of whom are former maquila workers, began creating new "assemblages of things," which afforded them an opportunity to reject the maquiladora sector altogether. One example of their assemblages of things to resist the devastating effects of neoliberalism is their construction of ecological toilets. Because the corporations and the Mexican government do not provide proper water and sanitation in the poor colónias where the majority of female maquiladora workers live, sanitation is a grave health hazard. The women, because of the lack of basic infrastructure, began creating ecological toilets. One member of Las Hormigas explains the project:

> We've been working on the eco-toilets for three years now. In this [free-trade] zone, we only have half a year with water. We have organized ourselves on this project. Before we had the toilets, we had outhouses, but a lot of animals would be there—worms, cockroaches; sometimes every two months we would have to change it and make a new hole. Also, with a lot of rain coming through, we would have these big floods. Imagine what happens to the latrine. It all comes out and goes everywhere. It's very unhealthy. The eco-toilets are good because they don't contaminate at all. You also don't have different types of animals coming in that carry diseases like black widows, which are commonly attracted to latrines. Apart from not contaminating, you can also use what's in it. It's like a compost . . . feces . . . you can use it as fertilizer . . . for trees or gardens, things like that—to help make this area less than a dusty desert. (Agustina, personal communication, November 3, 2005)

In conjunction with a local Catholic organization, the Sisters of Tonatzín, community members have begun selling their toilets to other Mexican and US customers. In their *re*assemblage of things, these women in Anapra have not only increased their safety, they have also improved their quality of life in numerous ways. Agustina continues:

> The main difference between working in a maquiladora and building the eco-toilets is the schedule. I used to leave at 2 p.m. in the afternoon and wouldn't return until 1 a.m. I used to go to bed at 2 a.m. and wake up at 6 a.m. to take the kids to school. I would have to do laundry, iron their clothes, and make dinner—and, again at 2 p.m., I would have to leave to work at the maquiladora. I used to get 420 pesos per week. It was about 40 US dollars per week. But now I decide my own schedule. I decide what days of the week I work. We have more time for our families and to learn other things. In the last two weeks, they [our old factory bosses] said: "Oh we made 100 pesos." I said, "No, that's what we pay ourselves; we are our own bosses." We have our own board that decides wages. It's an advantage. We see the money that comes in, and we decide how to distribute it, and what to buy. It has changed my life. The work at the maquiladoras is *very* tedious—very boring. We do the same thing over and over again. What we do here sometimes is rotate tasks, so there are different places and things to work on. (Personal communication, November 5, 2005; emphasis in original)[11]

CONCLUDING REMARKS

This chapter's analysis of the "assemblage of things" on the assembly line of the maquiladoras in the world's largest free-trade zone troubles Bennett's (2005) "enchantment" with the "assemblage of things" by demonstrating the problematics of a new materialist position that assigns equal weight and value to human and nonhuman things in the realm of agency. I contend that Bennett (2005) is able to adopt the position of "enchantment" over, say, the view of exploitation because new materialist theorizing lacks a critical contextualization of said

---

11. I met with members of Las Hormigas during each of my visits to Juárez during the period 2003–2008. In 2016 I was unable to meet with them. However, I was able to ascertain that their ecological toilet business, as well as their food co-op and community garden, continues to grow exponentially. Additionally, by highlighting the success of Las Hormigas, I by no means suggest that the unions and maquiladora workers should not continue to organize to improve their own working conditions.

things. There is always a history of how things are assembled, and that history cannot be severed from the context of those things within neoliberal capitalism. The utility in examining the assemblages of things through the lens of neoliberalism is the ability to examine the conditions in which the things are assembled, and for whose benefit.

New materialists' radical displacement of the human subject disallows analysis of how the assemblage of things pertains to the effect of these assemblages on bodies and communities. As this chapter has demonstrated, the assemblage of things is never neutral and thus cannot be isolated in its properties and impacts. Bennett (2005) attempts to forestall a neoliberal capitalist critique by stating that things like American imperialism and corporate greed are merely "one factor" and "are not the sole or necessarily the most profound actant in the assemblage in play" (p. 464). Bennett's (2005) easy dismissal of market forces erases those things' history and purpose. If we turn our attention back to the assemblages of things on the assembly line inside the maquiladoras within the free-trade zone of Ciudad Juárez, we see that the dispersal of agency is not neutral. The assemblage of roads and lights, for example, is solely for the corporations' own interests. Similarly, the pregnancy sticks are provided not for the sake of women's reproductive health but, instead, to measure a woman's productivity—or lack thereof—on the assembly line. Examining the economic structure in Juárez has proved that neoliberal capitalism's role in the assemblage of things *is* the most profound—and, I would add, deadly–actant. Neoliberal logic drives where things are situated, whom they affect, and the lived experiences of these assembled things' effects on bodies.

The new materialist position attempts to challenge this notion by leveraging the claim that "because each member-actant maintains an energetic pulse slightly 'off' from that excluded by the assemblage, such assemblages are never fixed blocks but open-ended wholes" (Bennett, 2005, p. 447). If we take the Las Hormigas project of the reassemblages of things in producing ecological toilets as a means of resistance to the exploitative labor conditions, certainly it is the female subject who drives this act of resistance. However, the female workers are not "excluded" from the larger system of assemblages. For instance, the female workers still rely on the maquiladora's discarding of material for their products and depend on the capitalist system to sell their goods.

What perhaps is most troubling if we are to adopt the ontology of the disbursement of agency in relation to the assemblages of things is Bennett's (2005) blaming of the victims who are forced to live within these larger systems—in this case, the victims of the feminicidios. At the end of her essay, she states:

> It is ultimately a manner of political judgment what is more needed today: should we acknowledge the distributive quality of agency in order to address the power of human–nonhuman assemblages and to resist a politics of blame? Or should we persist with a strategic understatement of material agency in the hope of enhancing the accountability of specific humans? (Bennett, 2005, p. 464)

If we concede the former argument and align with the latter position, an understanding of how the neoliberal capitalist systems of free trade and corporate interest function to produce feminicidios is not only left out of the equation; the feminicidios, hazardous working conditions, and exploitation become the problem that the women themselves are left to solve. There is no structural accountability. Instead, what the female maquiladora workers demand is for the corporations and the Mexican and US governments to be accountable to the *humans*—the *women* whose bodies are exploited and discarded as a result of the deadly conditions within the free-trade zone.

Finally, this chapter has spoken back to new materialist theorists who seek the answer to the question "how does recognition of the nonhuman and nonindividuated dimensions of agency alter established notions of moral responsibility and political accountability?" (Bennett, 2005, p. 446). This question, posed by Bennett (2005), is an important one. In the new materialists' disregarding of neoliberal capitalism, the state-corporate role in the perpetuation of slave labor wages, the gendered patterns of discrimination on women's bodies, the lack of public infrastructure and safety measures, and treacherous living conditions are exempt from interrogation. We are unable to assess how these neoliberal capitalist practices not only give rise to but also perpetuate feminicidio. And there is nothing enchanting about that.

CHAPTER 3

Feminicidio, Public Memory, and "Thing Power"

This pink cross is to remind the authorities that the feminicidio of
my daughter Gloria remains unpunished, almost three years after
they found her thrown here in the middle of rubble and trash.

—MARIA ANGELINA TARANGO RONQUILLO, MOTHER OF
GLORIA, PERSONAL COMMUNICATION, JANUARY 3, 2005

THE PURPOSE of this chapter is to interrogate the new materialist theoretical concept of "thing power." The turn towards inanimate objects,
first advanced by Latour (1999) and extended more recently in the
works of Pflugfelder (2015) and Barnett and Boyle (2010), contends that
inanimate objects such as hop plants, bicycle paths, speed bumps, and
beer hops all contain inherent persuasive properties. "Thing-power"
suggests that objects are not simply inert tools but are *themselves*
vibrant agents of measurable power. I contend that the turn towards
objects in assessment of materiality is indeed an important theoretical
move. However, "thing power," as currently theorized by new materialists, because of its lack of attention to political power structures and
larger cultural hegemonic discourses is theoretically inadequate.

Moreover, I contend that things are afforded their power only
through the mediation of rhetoric instigated by human agency for strategic purposes. To make my case, I enact a rhetorical analysis of the
Mexican government's feminicidio monuments in relation to studies
of public memory. I then demonstrate how things, deployed by human
agency and mediated through rhetoric, function as "matter-memory-
makers"—things that strategically challenge hegemonic constructions
of feminicidio victims while acting as warnings for other women and

girls. I first analyze the Mexican government's hegemonic feminicidio monuments, then examine the family members' and activists' strategic deployment of things in order to challenge state hegemonic constructions, and call on the public to act in the searches for the disappeared women and girls. Finally, in this chapter I offer examples for how the strategic deployment of things, enacted by the family members and activists, can transform place and space to challenge a public's cultural perceptions and meanings of the feminicidios. Analysis of matter in this chapter includes telephone poles, paint, cardboard, concrete, wood, park benches, and trash receptacles.

MEXICAN GOVERNMENT MONUMENTS

As pointed out, because of the circulation of two dominant hegemonic state narratives—"the dark myth" coupled with "business as usual"—the Mothers and activists are engaging in ongoing rhetorical work to disrupt these logics. Currently, the Mothers and activists are in a perpetual process of marking feminicidio through two dominant counter-hegemonic strategies: painting pink crosses to demarcate the locations where women's bodies have been found, and using wood to erect pink crosses in strategic locations as permanent forms of protest. Through an analysis of these two ongoing and distinct discursive strategies and tactics, I demonstrate how the state's process of "mnemonicide" (Morris, 2004)—the suppression and erasure of memories through the official state feminicidio monument, as well as dominant discourse—is countered through the family members' and activists' transformation of place and space through the implementation of what I call "matter-memory-makers."

According to Phillips (2004), analysis of public memory can be framed in two ways: "the memory of publics" and "the publicness of memory" (p. 3). This chapter interrogates these framings of memory by first analyzing the hegemonic constructions of the feminicidio victims embedded within the Mexican government's monument, and then analyzing how the family members of the feminicidio victims use things to make their daughters' memories matter. We will first examine the official government "cotton field" monument.

As previously cited, the Inter-American Court of Human Rights ruled that the Mexican government must erect a public monument in remembrance of the Juárez feminicidios. In 2011 the government built the "cotton field" monument on the site where the eight infamous feminicidio victims were found. On the ten-year anniversary of the cotton-field feminicidio discoveries, the government held the "unveiling" ceremony. To protest the government's lack of investigations and failure to end the impunity surrounding the feminicidios, many of the Mothers refused to attend the public commemoration ceremony. In addition to boycotting the commemoration, most of the victims' Mothers, to this day, refuse to visit the site. A Juárez activist explains why the Mothers and family members do not wish to visit the government-erected monument:

> When you go to the monument—it was 16 million pesos—Horrible! Horrible! Oh! 16 million pesos for that monument! And you know what, it's all wrong . . . the names are doubled, four of the names are girls who are missing still, there are a lot of names missing on the wall. Everything was done wrong. So we don't go there. It's like an insult to us. Why do we want that statue anyway? We need patrol cars! We need investigations! We need real serious things—not a monument that everybody goes to take a picture. No, no, no! (V. Caraveo, personal communication, June 28, 2016)

As Blair, Jeppeson, and Pucci (1991) remind us, "conflicts over whom or what to memorialize and in what ways have occurred frequently, and these conflicts often are registers of present and future political concern" (p. 263). In the instance of the official Juárez feminicidio monument, we have a unique opportunity to address the question of "forced remembrance" in conjunction with grassroots "matter-memory-making," in relation to theories of materiality and public memory studies. In conducting a rhetorical analysis of the "cotton field" monument, I contend that the memorial's material features, rather than commemorating the state-corporate crimes, engage in a politics of mnemonicide (Morris, 2004).

The "cotton field" monument stands at the precise location where the eight bodies of feminicidio victims were discovered. Prior to its erection, eight pink wooden crosses, erected by the Mothers, marked

their daughter's graves. For many years, family members and supporters of the justice movement would visit this sacred cite and bring flowers, photographs, and other materials of remembrance. Of significance,
the Mothers routinely used this sacred site for press conferences and
to commemorate the deaths of their daughters during protest events.
Care, throughout the years, was taken to ensure that the crosses' paint
remained bright pink and that the girls' names were always observable
to the public. The Mothers' monument was visible to all members of
the public at one of Ciudad Juárez's busiest traffic intersections. Juárenses were unable to drive or walk by the cotton field without being
reminded of the feminicidios that occurred.

Unlike the pre-existing Mothers' monument, the government's
"public" monument is anything but public. The memorial is enclosed by
three high walls and fitted with a gate. For Juárenses driving or walking
by, it is impossible to view the memorial from its exterior walls. There
is no signage on the streets, or on the structure itself, to alert the public
to its existence. Likewise, the memorial's walls occlude the feminicidio
monument from those who traverse through the main thoroughfare.

Because of this visual obstruction, rather than calling attention to
the state's culpability in the women's murders, the Mexican government
enacts a "politics of forgetting" (Vivian, 2004). One feminicidio activist
explains the problematic of this physical occlusion:

> The monument is private and enclosed. There's limited access [to it],
> so there are very few people who go and view it. There is not much
> access to it, and it seems that they [Mexican government] did it just
> to do it, but not for a real cause or purpose. Making feminicidio vis-
> ible is very important because that is a preventative measure. If young
> women aren't aware of how other women have disappeared, then they
> might not be able to prevent this from happening. (M. Ortiz, personal
> communication, June 19, 2016)

Indeed, as Haskins (2011) reminds us, monuments are "often
designed not so much to promote remembrance of past events as to fix
present cultural norms and power relations" (p. 49). Upon entering the
gates, visitors are confronted with three high walls and a long barren
pathway. Along each side of the long walls are six-foot encasements,
stretching the perimeter's borders. One encasement houses the names

FIGURE 3.1. Government feminicidio monument plaque. This image depicts the "unfinished" encasement. Photo taken by author, Ciudad Juárez, 2016.

of the "cotton field" feminicidio victims. However, as pointed out by former mayoral candidate Vicky Caraveo, the remembrance is riddled with errors, including misspelled names, absent names, and names in duplicate. As Haskins (2011) also points out, because monuments are expressions of particular ideologies, they have the capacity to function as "material manifestations of hegemonic national narratives" (p. 48). In this instance, the lives of the women in Juárez are indeed not worthy of public remembrance.

In addition to the posthumous gross errors, notably, the encasement is not finished—there exists a plethora of empty space next to the already designated names. Extending beyond the first plaque holder, the other enshrined casings all remain empty—spaces yet to be filled. These unfinished spaces, I assert, represent the potentially thousands of bodies yet to be found and identified.

Additionally, because the monument's physical space grossly exceeds the space necessary to commemorate the cotton field murders, it can be read, symbolically, as the representation of *future* murders—feminicidios that are inevitably waiting to occur—their symbolic space already solidified and "in waiting." The walls' repositories can plainly hold thousands of more name plaques. Thus, the monument can be read not only as a failed commemoration but as a warning about where women who "act out" will end up. Vivian (2004) describes how these physical-monument properties function as "unfinished memory work" (p. 204)—in this instance, that of the physical act of future feminicidios. Irma González, head of the Juárez Women's Institute, confirms this premise:

> There are other measures that have to do more with preventative actions than with commemoration actions. Like the memorial you saw at the cotton field—where at the end of the day . . . it is supposed to serve as a constant reminder that these crimes took place here and that they cannot continue to happen. It's a measure to avoid this to continue—to repeat itself—a measure to eradicate the problem, to not allow it to continue. What we don't want is for more women to get murdered, for more women to disappear. That's the significance of that memorial—to construct a collective memory of these crimes in this city . . . to mark our history . . . so that these sorts of things cannot happen again. Unfortunately, this hasn't been possible because this memorial was inaugurated in March of 2011 and, that February, various remains were found in a town nearby of women who lived in our city and were moved to that remote area. It was far from a busier town—it was an isolated area. To this day, 24 women have been identified in that area—more than the remains found in the cotton fields. (I. Vargas, personal communication, June 21, 2016)

Thus, although as Biesecker's (2002) work in memory studies contends, memorials can symbolically construct the meaning of a corpus in the public imaginary (pp. 212–13). In Juárez, while the memorial's meaning is of course critical for public awareness and remembrance of these state crimes—for the Mothers, the primary telos is not the *symbolic* construction of a corpus; it is for the state to produce the *material* corpses and remains of their missing daughters.

"MATTER-MEMORY-MAKERS"

Like the Mothers of the Argentinean disappeared who protested weekly in the town square of Plaza de Mayo, in the late 1990s (Foss &

Domenici, 2001), in Juárez, when bodies of victims began to appear, and many young women began to go missing, a small group of Mothers gathered the first Thursday of each month in front of the state attorney general's office to protest the lack of investigations into their daughters' deaths and disappearances (Corchado, 2007). However, as detailed in chapters 1 and 2, due to the necessity of often having to work at a maquiladora or to care for their children—coupled with the Mexican government's strategies of intimidation and harassment—the Mothers were not always able or willing to embody an ongoing physical presence of protest: "We ask ourselves: what else can we do? Are we going to have to be there all the time . . . standing in front of them . . . constantly demanding that they continue searching for our daughters?" (J. Luís, personal communication, June 25, 2016). Undeterred, the family members began using pink and black crosses as synecdochic representations of their agitating bodies. Indeed, as Zelizer (2002) reminds us: "the material object has long been seen as a stand-in or synecdochic representation of larger events, issues, and settings" (p. 157).

Pink and black crosses began emerging in Juárez, to announce and denounce feminicidio, in the 1990s (Maria Angelina Tarango Ronquillo, personal communication, January 3, 2005). As Blair, Dickinson, and Ott (2010) have demonstrated, symbols of memory production are often "activated by present concerns, issues, or anxieties" (p. 6). The Mothers began painting black crosses on pink backgrounds on telephone poles throughout the city and erecting wooden pink-painted crosses in front of important government buildings, such as the fiscalía [prosecutor's office]. Paula Flores, Mother of feminicidio victim Sagrario Gonzalez, and one of the founding members of Voces sin Echo [Voices in Echo], articulates the meaning of the colors of the crosses:

The pink base represents women, and the black cross represents the loss of their daughters. In addition to the long-standing monument at the border, along with the wooden crosses that are permanently placed in front of government buildings, other monuments are placed strategically at the sites where the victims' bodies have been found. This activity keeps alive the memories of our daughters, and is a message to the Mexican authorities that we continue to seek justice. (Personal communication, June 25, 2016)

FIGURE 3.2. Pink crosses. The pink crosses, erected by the Mothers, function as a form of permanent protest outside of the fiscalía [prosecutor] offices. Photo taken by author, Ciudad Juárez, 2016.

Once the Mothers had a symbol for the movement, in 1997 they began deploying the crosses in strategic places throughout the city. Feminicidio activist Alma Gómez details this history:

> In 1997, the Mothers began organizing. One of our first public actions was to raise public awareness around the feminicidios. We painted 168 crosses throughout the city—on telephone poles along the Camino Real Highway to denounce the feminicidios. We then extended this strategy to various other actions—including placing crosses in front of the governor's palace in Chihuahua, and other key governmental buildings in Ciudad Juárez. (Personal communication, November 1, 2005)[1]

The pink crosses, then, because of their placement directly in front of the government buildings, "speak" to the authorities in "political and deliberative" fashion (Blair et al., 1991, p. 263). Of significance is that

---

1. Mothers have also erected crosses in the colónia of Anapra, and in the Arroyo de Navajo valley, where mass graves of feminicidio bodies have been found.

on multiple occasions, the crosses that the Mothers erected have been vandalized, removed, and even burned to the ground. Alma Gómez recounts the history of the cross placed in front of the Chihuahua governor's palace:

> Apparently, there were some people who stole the first cross. Also, the first one . . . that one was burned down. But when they [officials] took it down, we told the governor that we would make a bigger one. We made a bigger one—and we told him that if he took this one down, we would come up with an even bigger one. That is why he did not take this one down. Since then, there have been many protests in support of the victims' families, each time adding nails onto the cross as a representation of their deaths. (Personal communication, November 3, 2005)

The process of adding nails to the monument performed the act of public mourning and ongoing commemoration of the women's deaths (Winter, 1995). In 2002 the Mothers organized a six-day march from Chihuahua to Juárez: "on March 8th through March 13th, to commemorate the feminicidios on International Women's Day, we marched it [the cross] from Chihuahua to Juárez to demand justice. This second cross now stands at the US–Mexico border" (A. Gómez, personal communication, November 3, 2005).

Through the Mothers' strategic placement of the crosses, I assert, the artifacts not only function to commemorate the feminicidios and function as promulgation for the movement—but also act as a cautionary tale to women. Indeed, as Phillips (2010) reminds us: "the rhetoric of public memory . . . can be understood as operating in different ways depending upon the level at which rhetorical appeals operate" (p. 219). In addition to the cross placed at the US–Mexico border, the Mothers erected crosses at the entry point of Chihuahua, Mexico. The placement of the crosses at these border sites—in particular the monument carried by the Mothers to the US–Mexico border—enacts Phillips and Reyes's (2011) contention that public memories can act as "'global memoryscapes'—to capture the intersection between memorial practices and global forces . . . moving across national boundaries, transported by individuals and technologies and the movement of these memories along a global landscape" (pp. 2, 19). Although Phillips and Reyes do not take a position on whether globalization is inherently positive or negative when advancing their "global memoryscapes" framing strategy, the Mothers' placement of the cross on the border, in no uncertain terms, indicts globalization, NAFTA, and free trade as culpable agents in relation to the feminicidios of the women of Ciudad Juárez. So, although Phillips (2010) contends that forms of public remembrance can be understood as "objects inserted into spaces of [pre-existing] memory" (p. 220), as demonstrated by the Mothers, it is the "insertion" of the *things* themselves—the wooden crosses at these border and government sites, in this instance—which *creates* memory spaces. As such, I contend, these objects function as "matter-memory-makers."

In addition to the pink crosses indicting neoliberal globalization's role in producing feminicidio, Patricia Cervantes, Mother of feminicidio victim Neyra, explains how the crosses respond to a cultural exigence—the need to warn women and girls about the inherent dangers of gendered violence in Ciudad Juárez:

> Every time I'd pass the crosses, I would avoid them because I didn't want to be there . . . regardless of how much I would try to avoid it, I'm here now. Those people, they think that their daughters are not in danger, but they are. Because the murderers roam free, here, in our streets. People don't realize that their daughters are in danger. But they are in danger! Because the same people who killed my daughter are free in the street. . . . I still feel my daughter's presence every time I pass the cross. (Personal communication, January 2, 2005)

As Biesecker (2002) argues: "collective memory *per se* [emphasis in original] is neither necessarily conservative nor innovative in force. Instead, the political entailments of collective memory are an effect of what and how we remember, and the *uses* [emphasis added] to which those memories are *put* [emphasis added]" (p. 406). In addition to erecting pink wooden crosses throughout the city, victims' family members and activists are also using pre-existing objects in the city to mark where the feminicidio victims' bodies are found. The week before I returned to Juárez, in June 2016, eight bodies were found in the Acequia Madre river canal. In working with the family members of the victims and the activists, we decided to paint crosses at this site. Señor Don José Luis explains why the family members wanted to paint the crosses at this particular location:

We have found eight dead women here in the last 15 days! Three were found right in front of here—in the Acequia Madre. We are planning to paint crosses all over the Acequia Madre . . . from here—six to seven blocks are where the killings happen. This is where they [the killers] dump the bodies. I think that it is more important that we paint all along the Acequia Madre because a lot of bodies have been found . . . like six or seven bodies have been found in these past few weeks . . . there are some crosses painted on the posts, but they aren't part of the Acequia Madre. So we should paint here. (Personal communication, June 25, 2016)

José Luis's analysis punctuates how "social movements contest and remake places while the places themselves contest and remake social structures" (Endres & Senda-Cook, 2011, p. 261).

He continues:

It's difficult to paint from the inside because of the houses, but is important to point out where the dead women were found. We need to climb down [the hill]. They were found right where we are, but at different parts of the river—all up and down the Acequia Madre. So, we should paint the posts next to the street of the Acequia. I was thinking of going from here to a block away. Why a block? Because that is where other trash is collected . . . over there is where they dump the bodies—with the city's trash. It is over there where these crimes are committed. So at the place where we stopped, it would be very easy to get in my truck and dump a body. Yes, in a flash! Not even a minute! So those are the things we notice. So if we don't paint here, they [the public] won't notice. If you noticed, though, there weren't many [telephone] posts, so we will have to paint on the main highway, the rocks, or on what's available. (J. Luis, personal communication, June 25, 2016)[2]

Thus, as evidenced in this example, the family members and activists, because of a lack of telephone poles, "made do" with the structural matter that existed: rocks and concrete: "We painted up and down the

---

2. We had to paint very quickly and could not stop, as we were in the "Barrio Azteca," where those responsible for the feminicidios live—their territory. While we were on the bridge scoping out the locations to paint, for instance, we heard a gunshot. José then said, "We'd better go. I'm a bit worried for you and myself."

FIGURE 3.3. Painting the riverbed. Señora Paula Flores, Mother of Sagrario, Señor José Luis Castillo, Father of Esmeralda, and Maclovio, painting the riverbed in the Acequia Madre canal, where, in June 2016, remains of eight feminicidios were found within a period of two weeks. They used cardboard and spray cans for stenciled messages. Photo taken by author, Ciudad Juárez, 2016.

rocks, mountain bed and the main highway adjacent to the riverbed, where the bodies were found" (J. Luis, personal communication, June 25, 2016). Hence, in this instance, not only did the family members and activists warn the women and girls in Juárez about the danger of walking along the riverbed, they also warned the Mexican government and the cartels that they knew how and where the bodies were being disposed of. José Luis explains the urgency of this transference of matter into a discursive warning:

> We are telling all young women that wherever they see these crosses, it means that they are in danger—no matter what time of day it is. It doesn't matter if it's noon. We are doing this because of the women they found here in the Acequia Madre. I am inviting the Mothers of those who have disappeared not to be silent, and to tell the government that we know, and that we won't say silent. (Personal communication, June 25, 2016)

Certainly, as Castiglia and Reed (2012) argue, memory is dynamic because it is inherently "incomplete, fragmented, affect-saturated, and . . . continually open to the imaginative process of rearticulation, reinvention, and adaption" (p. 43). So, while the government monument functions hegemonically to silence, forget—and "misremember" (Phillips, 2010)—the family members' and activists' public monuments, through the utilization of various types of matter, function counterhegemonically to commemorate, promulgate, agitate, and alert.

THINGS' TRANSFORMATION OF SPACE AND PLACE

As demonstrated, while the objects of telephone poles, riverbed walls, rocks, and cardboard are installed as matter-memory-makers, the state continues to attempt to "unmake" these memories in specific places and spaces. The role of the Mexican government, in relation to the Mothers' memory-making, is, as demonstrated in chapters 1 and 2, always subjected to the neoliberal logics of the state. Currently, because the Mexican government's project of feminicidio memory unmaking is driven by tourist capital, the government's "unmaking" is taking place not in the barrios but in the tourist zones. Jessica Morales, feminicidio activist and member of Frenté Marginal, explains:

Obviously, the crosses and the missing posters are going to taint what they [Mexican government and corporations] want to show in Juárez. They [authorities] want to send the message that everything is better—and that they don't kill women anymore—and none of them [the women] are disappearing. But the women who get out of school at 8 p.m. and have to cross here, in the center, don't really have a choice—just like the maquiladora workers. This "tourist" zone is a very dangerous place. The most convenient thing to do is to carry scissors or a knife to defend yourself with. But last year, for example, Juan Gabriel came here, and the governor of Chihuahua César Duarte, and Enrique Serrano, president of the municipality, inaugurated a mural of the singer . . . so, for that event, they took everything down [missing posters] and painted over the crosses. There were conflicts because the Mothers wanted to speak and let them know that their daughters aren't urban legends—that they aren't a myth here in Juárez . . . the Mothers came back, after the authorities removed them, and painted the crosses again. (Personal communication, June 24, 2016)

The state-corporate feminicidio memories must be suppressed so that tourism can return to Juárez:

> Before [people knew about the feminicidios], a lot of businesses, like the bars, were closing because they were losing money. I think that many [people] still don't have much confidence that things are now good here in Juárez . . . but with the new advertisements, more people are beginning to come on Fridays—on Saturdays—to dance . . . and to drink. But before, no. The youth didn't come out. (N. Hernandez, personal communication, 2016)

Recently, for example, in an attempt to restart the tourist sector, a Juárez corporation launched the "Be Proud to Be from Juárez" campaign, which touts Juárez as the city "just as beautiful as New York or Paris" (Commercial-El Paso, 2015). The state erected dancing water fountains where many of the girls disappear, in addition to giving the shopping centers an aesthetic superficial face-lift.[3] Indeed, social space "is determined economically by capital . . . and ruled politically by the State" (Lefebvre, 1991, p. 227). Space, in other words, is always interpellated by hegemonic logics. José Luis, recognizing that the state logic of tourist-capitalism was what was driving the removal of the feminicidio and missing posters, began repurposing various forms of matter within the tourist spaces, to counteract this state hegemony. The first things that were rearticulated were shopping-mall directories—thereby taking the matter-memory-making directly to the site of capital consumption:

> I post things up in the center, and sometimes we have to run away because the police end up chasing us. But that is where I want to post the picture of my daughter. It doesn't matter that they made the center "clean" and developed it for restaurants and bars. I want to post her

---

3. In an attempt to draw more tourists from the El Paso area, the Mexican government installed water fountains on the main street of town. Of course, colónias, such as Anapra, still lack access to basic water and sanitation services. This street is also one of the main streets where the girls are known to disappear.

picture right *there* because people will see it while they are shopping. (J. Luis, personal communication, June 22, 2016; emphasis in original)

When shoppers turn to the directory to search for the location of shoes, or pants or jackets, they find themselves, instead, searching for Esmeralda, one of the disappeared.[4]

By manipulating matter—in this case, turning shopping-mall directories into maps for missing bodies—the family members effectively transform the social space. As Lefebvre (1991) explains: "A social space contains a great diversity of objects . . . both natural and social . . . such 'objects' are thus not only things but also relations" (p. 77). A space typically used for the relations of production—the consumption of goods—is transformed into a newly articulated plane of relations—one where the logic of tourist-capitalism is exposed, and effectively tied to the logic of state-corporate feminicidio. Consequently, the social space's meaning in Juárez is transformed through the rearticulation of the assemblage of things, which I call "practiced matter." As Lefebvre (1991) states: "The form of social space is encounter, assembly, simultaneity. But what assembles, or what is assembled? The answer is: everything that there is *in space*, everything that is produced either by nature or by society . . . things, objects, works, signs and symbols" (p. 101; emphasis in original). Consequently, these objects function to counter the hegemonic logics of "state-corporate" feminicidios and tourist-capitalism. In addition to the rearticulated store directories, consumer tourist and shopping spaces are also transformed through the "matter-memory-making" of bus stops and trash receptacles. As Lluvia Rocha explains:

We decided to paint the bus stop bench pink with the black cross to symbolize disappearances, because no one is ever sitting there. Also, we wanted to do trash cans, because many of the women's bodies have been found dumped in trash cans. So, that is the significance of these two elements—the bench and the trash can. Another important thing: the bench and the trash cans are the property of the municipality.

---

4. In addition to the missing posters of Esmeralda and Silvia Elena, a sign for Lilia Alejandra García Andrade was erected on February 14, 2015, in front of the building in Ciudad Juárez where her tortured and murdered body was found.

FIGURE 3.4. Missing poster advertisement. Señor José Luis transformed this shopping directory into a large missing-poster advertisement. It is located in the main shopping district in the center of Ciudad Juárez. Photo taken by author, Ciudad Juárez, 2016.

No one has touched them, and it's been a month and a half since we painted them. (Personal communication, June 20, 2016)

As Shome (2003) reminds us, space is a "product of relations that are themselves active and constantly changing material practices through which it comes into being" (p. 41). In other words, spatial meaning is a continual process of active production—in this case, through the rearticulation of matter that functions to reconfigure the space's meaning, and perhaps even its purpose. As Lefebvre (1991) has theorized:

Space is at once result and cause, product and producer; it is also a *stake*, the locus of projects and actions deployed as part of specific strategies, and hence also the object of *wagers* on the future—wagers which are articulated, if never completely. (pp. 142–143; emphasis in original)

In Ciudad Juárez, the Mothers, Fathers, and activists continue to wager that the repurposing of objects through a new spatial analytic, to mark the feminicidios as real, and not a dark myth, will disrupt the dominant state-corporate logic of tourist capital driving and perpetuating the ongoing mnemocide of the feminicidios.

CONCLUDING OBSERVATIONS

This chapter has sought to highlight the significance of the deployment and redeployment of matter, through human agency, to attain specific rhetorical goals. There are several important contributions in this chapter for scholar-activists to consider. First, my analysis of matter as "memory makers" has important contributions for future work analyzing matter and its various relationships to articulations of public memory. As demonstrated, future political projects may want to consider the role of "practiced matter" in bringing a memory to a public's consciousness, rather than merely analyzing the matter that already exists in its current historical iterations.

Further, as demonstrated, the memories that are invoked through matter do not simply commemorate; they also simultaneously function as a call to action. When family members and activists mark the border as a site where the disappeared women and girls are being circulated, or paint the rocks and concrete where the bodies are being dumped, the feminicidio victims are not just simply remembered, they are ascribed with a history—and, consequently, members of publics are provided specific directives for how to respond and act. For example, the aforementioned analyzed "memory-makers" call upon women and girls to take precautions whenever they come face-to-face with the pink crosses. Likewise, the strategic placement of the crosses in the riverbed and concrete walls denote a place for the public and family members to search.

This chapter also has important implications for thinking not simply about how things are assembled but also how, through human agency, individuals and groups can *re*assemble matter into efficacious political projects. The power of the families' "matter-memory-makers" of shopping directories, bus benches, and trash receptacles, for example, utilize matter with an a-priori purpose and redeploy it to challenge current meanings, and to generate new meanings altogether. As demonstrated, the logics of neoliberal consumerism and state-corporate tourist capital are radically refigured through matter's strategic reconfigurations. Thus, scholar-activists should be attending to matter of "the everyday" with a careful eye toward utilizing pre-existing objects for different political ends. In sum, in stark contrast to the new materialist position, reviewed in the introductory chapter, purporting that matter has inherent agentic properties, as this chapter has established, the role of human agency in "practiced matter" is indeed what affords matter and objects their ability to "kick back" at neoliberal hegemonic logics.

PLATE 1. The historic moment when the International Caravan for Justice culminated in a joint protest at the US–Mexico border bridge

PLATE 2. Pink crosses erected at the entrance of the main highway into Chihuahua

PLATE 3. Feminicidio memorial cross, which stands directly at the US–Mexico border

PLATE 4. Evidence of armed physical government military intimidation, harassment, and surveillance during the rastreo [search]

PLATE 5. "Las Hormigas" ecological toilets

PLATE 6. One of the hidden rooms in one of the bars on the main promenade of Ciudad Juárez where forced prostitution occurs

PLATE 7. The largest cemetery in Ciudad Juárez

PLATE 8. Flyer circulated to publicize the "Arroyo del Navajo" rastreo [Navajo Riverbed search] for victims' remains

PLATE 9. Pink crosses erected by family members at the location of the Arroyo del Navajo [Navajo Riverbed] to mark the mass gravesite of feminicidio remains

PLATE 10. Image of the dancing water fountains installed by the government

PLATE 11. Marking of a site where remains were found during the rastreos [searches] for feminicidio remains in the Arroyo del Navajo [Navajo Riverbed]

PLATE 12. Señor José Luís searching for his daughter

PLATE 13. Evangelina Arce, Mother of Silvia, keeps this collection
of her personal artifacts from the movement

CHAPTER 4

Feminicidio, Objects, and Affect

THIS CHAPTER'S GOAL is to connect the new materialist literature concerning object-oriented ontologies (Bryant, 2011) with a pairing of rhetorical affect studies. The chapter stresses the importance of not viewing objects as inherently persuasive but as imbued with meaning through strategic acts of human agency. It seeks to understand how, when bodies and objects come together, affective properties may be activated to propel agents to act. To bring these currently disparate bodies of literature together, I use the Juárez "Faces of Feminicidio" mural project as a text. The project was cofounded by Lluvia Rocho and Maclovio, and sparked by Esmeralda's Father, José Luis. The "Faces of Feminicidio" originated in 2010, during the "lost years"—the third wave of violence. The project was born out of necessity—in response to the Mexican government's routine destruction of the missing girls' posters and erasure and removal of the pink crosses.

José Luis explains:

The mural idea came about because they [authorities] took away the missing posters, and painted over our crosses in the business areas. So, when people would pass by, they would think that there were no missing women anymore—or that they [authorities] found them all! That gave us great fear because young women would think everything was alright, and lower their guards. They also wouldn't let us post missing posters in the center of Juárez, or any other info. So, we started to organize. We spoke to Maclovio and Lluvia, and they told us that they knew how to draw. We asked for their help, and they agreed. We had the workers—the help and painters—but we didn't have the paint. So we did an exchange of tacos for spray cans. And that is how we started to paint murals. (Personal communication, June 21, 2016)

Maclovio details how he began painting the victims' faces:

So, yeah, he [José Luis] gave an interview and said that we were going to do 100 portraits! So, we said yes, but we didn't know when they would be completed. He just said, "If you want to do it, start with 100!" We were like, "Okaaaay" [laughing]. The second interview he gave, he said 130. We said, "Okaaaay." Now he says the goal is 180. We don't know when we will finish, but we will do it. So now we have this agreement. So, since then, we have been doing various works like selling popsicles and tacos on the street to pay for the paints. (Personal communication, June 25, 2016)

The "faces of feminicidio" is a collaborative effort between the artists, activists, and the family members of the murdered and disappeared. Before paining a feminicidio victim's face, Lluvia and Maclovio interview the Mothers and family members so that they can learn about the victims' lives. Questions often asked by Lluvia include "What were some of your daughter's dreams and aspirations?" and "What were some of your daughter's favorite things—what did she enjoy doing?" and "How would you like your daughter's life represented and remembered?" In addition, Lluvia and Maclovio always ask *where* the Mothers would like the mural to be located. Through the use of spray cans, paint, brushes, dwellings, and walls, used during the construction of each of the murals, Maclovio focuses on the victims' faces.

As of this writing, Maclovio and Lluvia have painted 21 murals and 26 faces. Eighteen of the murals are in Ciudad Juárez, one is located in Zacatétas, and one is in Mexico City. The question, then, of course, is why do the authorities continue to tear down and cover up the crosses and disappeared posters, but not deface or paint over the victims'

"Faces of Feminicidio" murals? I contend that it is because the murals perform a "haunting" of the state, function as protectors—"guardians of the barrio"—and provide emotive release for the Mothers' mourning through what I identify as "object-oriented affect." Objects analyzed in this chapter include spray paint, brushes, homes, walls, and buildings.

HAUNTING

Foss and Domenici (2001), in their analysis of the Mothers of Plaza de Mayo, argue that the metaphor of haunting "provides a useful rhetorical frame in which to understand the Mothers' actions" (p. 240). While Foss and Domenici assert that the Argentinian Mothers' strategies of haunting fostered "an experiencing of the presence of a disembodied spirit in a form that transcends boundaries of time and space" (p. 240), I contend, in this instance, that the murals' victims' faces haunt, protect, and comfort vis-á-vis the public's tactile interaction with the objects' location to the feminicidios in strategically situated places.

To theorize object-oriented affect, I conduct an analysis of the "Faces of Feminicidio" murals, using Levinas's (1985) trope of "the face," read through Gordon's (2008) theorizing of symbolic strategies of "haunting." As Gordon (2008) has demonstrated, haunting is an experiential modality that functions "as an animated state in which a repressed or unresolved social violence is making itself known" (p. xvi). I proceed, first, by detailing nine of the 21 murals.[1]

Marisela Escobedo

Marisela, Mother of Ruby, as mentioned in chapter 3, was assassinated by the state while protesting in front of the Chihuahua governor's palace. Marisela would often protest in mere undergarments—wearing only an image of her daughter cloaking her body to symbolize that the

---

1. In moving the academic discussion forward on new materialisms, I chose to analyze the murals which most poignantly represent various theoretical arguments. Analyzing only several is in no way, however, meant to privilege one life over another. To view the complete catalog of the murals, and to learn more about the "Faces of Feminicidio" project, visit Lluvia Rocha's ongoing blog at https://losrostrosdelfeminicidio. wordpress.com/

government had taken everything from her—that she had nothing left. Lluvia details the significance of painting Marisela:

> On the eve of Dia de los Muertos [Day of the Dead], we decided to paint a new mural in the neighborhood of Tepito on Montebello Street. This is a posthumous tribute to one of the most recognized national activists. Marisela Escobedo Ortiz was born in 1958. She was a social activist murdered in front of the Government Palace of Chihuahua, on the 16th of December, 2010, while demanding justice for the murder of her daughter, Ruby Marisol. Today, Marisela Escobedo has become a symbol of struggle against feminicidio. We decided to make this humble tribute to a great woman—a Mother who fought tirelessly to find justice for her daughter. (L. Rocha, personal communication, June 20, 2016)

Levinas (1982), when speaking of the human subject, argues that a human being's worth is unique and impossible to replace: "No one could replace me. In fact, it is a matter of saying the very identity of the human 'I' starting from this position or deposition of the sovereign 'I' . . . is a supreme dignity of the unique. 'I' am 'I' in the sole measure that 'I' am responsible, a non-interchangeable" (pp. 100–101). The state took Marisela—and while her physical presence is "nontransferable," her spirit is transferred through her haunting of the state via her ceaseless cries for justice.

Esmeralda, Rose, and Adriana

The second mural, depicting feminicidio victims Esmeralda Castillo, Rose Virginia Hernández Cano, and Adriana Sarmiento, is located in Ciudad Juárez in the area of Vicente Guerrero. It is a gigantic mural—covering the walls of two large adjacent apartment buildings. Lluvia explains the history of Esmeralda, Rose, and Adriana's mural:

> This mural includes the faces of Esmeralda Castillo, Adriana Sarmiento, and the portrait of Rosa Virginia Hernández Cano. All of them were feminicidio victims—well, there's a piece of bone of a leg [a femur] of Esmeralda, but José Luis hasn't accepted the DNA test. We worked for two weeks. We were nine people working on this mural—all street art-

ists—some of them were activists too. Paula Flores was there helping us out. We worked for two weeks in the summer.[2] Part of the mural represents women trafficking. That's why we put the international bridge alongside the flags of Mexico and the US. The Mexican flag has a pink cross in the center, and the US flag becomes like a war jet on a landing strip. On the American side, there are five soldiers and a crocodile with an Uncle Sam hat. On the Mexican side, there is Arroyo del Navajo [Riverbed of Navajo] in the background. We put a lot of pink crosses all over the place—and the letters of "¡Ni Una Más!" in the middle. The mural also has a character . . . the "maqui-loca."[3] It's a character that represents a factory worker who is a woman. So he painted her crossing the Rio Bravo with her passport and her visa. What we are arguing is that everyone says, "The feminicidios are a problem of Mexico." But, no! The US is responsible for NAFTA, and most of the corporations are US-owned multinational corporations. So, it's important to show how the US is guilty—just like Mexico, but people don't talk about the United States' role in the feminicidios. So that's something important that this mural represents. (L. Rocha, personal communication, June 20, 2016)

Levinas (1982) contends that the "face" is tied to societal discourse and structures: "Certainly. Face and discourse are tied. The face speaks. It speaks, it is in this that it renders possible and begins all discourse . . . and, more exactly, response or responsibility which is this authentic relationship" (pp. 87–88). Through this mural, the victims' faces haunt the discourses of capitalism and US imperialism. Moreover, because Gordon (2008) argues that haunting strategies produce cultural awareness of historical materialist hegemonic influences—the victims' faces, by looking directly at NAFTA, consequently haunt neoliberalism itself as a culpable agent.

---

2. Most of the murals were painted in the extreme temperatures of the desert heat.

3. The "maqui-loca" is a hegemonic construction, in the vernacular of Juárez, which depicts female factory workers as "loco" [crazy]. This discursive construction, of course, participates in the logic that the factory workers played a role, through their "wild and crazy behaviors," in their deaths. The "maqui-loca" figure has also been portrayed in several Juárez comic books.

FIGURE 4.1. Mural of US role in feminicidio. The mural's faces include Esmeralda Castillo, Rose Virginia Hernández Cano, and Adriana Sarmiento. The mural is located in Ciudad Juárez in Vicente Guerrero. Photo taken by author, Ciudad Juárez, 2016.

FIGURE 4.2. Mural of Monica Alanis. The mural is located at the Autonomous University in Ciudad Juárez. Photo taken by author, Ciudad Juárez, 2016.

Monica

Monica Alanis was attending college when she disappeared. Lluvia explains Monica's face:

> In June we [Maclovio and I] painted Monica Alanis. We had painted her before. She disappeared from the Autonomous University in Ciudad Juárez, so we painted her face in front of that university. We thought to ourselves, this is our opportunity to paint Monica at the very site where she disappeared. It was a very small wall, so we only painted her eyes. Monica's eyes were like beautiful big almonds—so right away you can recognize her likeness—her eyes, her eyebrows, and her hair. We also added a caption on the wall that says "Monica Alanis, student of Administration, last seen here in 2009." Don Ricardo Alanis, Monica's Father, was very grateful that we painted his daughter there. (L. Rocha, personal communication, June 20, 2016)

The muralists' focus on Monica's eyes, in concert with the articulation of where she was last seen, argues enthymematically that the public has a responsibility to act. As Levinas (1982) states, "I think that access to the face is straightaway ethical . . . when you see a nose, eyes, a forehead, a chin, and you can describe them . . . the skin of the face is that which stays most naked, most destitute . . . the face" (pp. 85–86). When members of the public lock eyes with Monica's eyes, the haunting exacted is one of an ethics that Levinas describes—an ethics of responsibility—to acknowledge Monica's death, and an obligation to search for her.

Mother Karla and Daughter Cinthia

In 2015 Lluvia and Maclovio painted Karla Castañeda and her daughter, one of the disappeared, Cinthia Jocabeth:

> We painted Karla near my house on a wall. This was on Antonio Caño-leto Street, in the Paulo Division. Their faces are painted on a wall on an abandoned street. Maclovio had promised Karla that he would paint her and her daughter at the Caminata Por La Vida [Walk for Life], in 2013. We know that Cinthia disappeared on the 24th of October, 2008—and, to this day, nothing is known of her whereabouts. Karla Castañeda is now in hiding because of the many death threats that she received from the Chihuahua governor, Caesar Duarte. After those threats, she fled to the US, with her four kids, seeking asylum. For these reasons, it was very important for us to paint Karla. We only painted the bottom of her face to represent her anonymity, because Karla's case has been one of the worst, in terms of her persecution. The state was going to kill Karla, due to her activism. So, if she didn't run away, they would have killed her, like Marisela Escobedo—so, that's why we decided to paint her this way. We also painted her wearing the mantle honoring her daughter. (L. Rocha, personal communication, June 20, 2016)

In this mural, as Lluvia describes, the public is unable to look into the Mother's eyes—we only see part of her face. Thus, the public recognizes, enthymematically, that because Karla is unable to search, the public must embody that responsibility; we must be her eyes. Levinas (1982) explains that when we encounter others' faces, we take on responsibility for their humanity. He explains, "I am responsible even for the *Other's responsibility*. These are extreme formulas which must not be detached from their context. In the concrete, many other

FIGURE 4.3. Mural of Karla Castañeda and Cinthia Jocabeth. The mural is located on Antonio Cañoleto Street, in the Paolo Division of Ciudad Juárez. Photo taken by author, Ciudad Juárez, 2016.

considerations intervene and require justice . . . but *justice* only has meaning if it retains the responsibility for the *other* man [*sic*]" (p. 99; emphases added). The public, therefore, is haunted into taking on the Mother's responsibility to search; we are all Cinthia's caretakers.

Maria Elena

Maria Elena's mural highlights the strategic use of symbols, which function to represent the girls' lives. Lluvia recounts important elements of Maria Elena's story:

Maria Elena disappeared in 2002. Her daughter was working cleaning houses. Her name is Maria Elena Chavez Caldera. Maria Elena worked in Nogales, a barrio near here. When she left work, she disappeared. Fifteen days before that, she got a new boyfriend. She started a relationship with a man who was older—much older than her—more than 10 years. He was about 30 years old, and she was only 15.

Julia, her Mother, thinks that that man had something to do with her daughter's disappearance. Six months ago, I interviewed her Mother, Julia, to learn more about Maria Elena's life, before we began painting the mural. Based upon what I learned, we are going to paint an elephant—like a ceramic elephant, because that was one of the gifts that Maria Elena gave to her Mother on Mother's Day. We will also paint roses, because that was another gift that Maria Elena gave to Julia. We must also paint a two-story house, because that was one of her [Maria Elena's] dreams—to build a two-story house for her to live with her Mother. (L. Rocha, personal communication, June 20, 2016)

When Maclovio and Lluvia paint symbols, in the mural, that represent specific aspects of the victims' lives and the futures taken from them, the face "haunts," through testifying to their material realness. Levinas (1982) argues that the face demands acknowledgment of its truth as a human subject: "The subject . . . says, 'here I am!' *testifies* to the Infinite. It is through this testimony . . . that the revelation of the Infinite occurs" (Levinas, 1982, p. 106; emphasis in original). Through Maria Elena's testimony of bringing her Mother gifts, and her plans to live in a two-story house, her life was not a "dark myth" but a tangible reality.

Sagrario

Sagrario Flores's mural is unique because of where it is located. Paula, Sagrario's Mother, requested that her daughter's mural cover their home. Lluvia explicates Sagrario's mural:

Sagrario's mural is a very special mural because we painted it on her house. Sagrario disappeared on April 16th, 2008, and her body was found two weeks later. She disappeared when she was working in a maquiladora, and she disappeared on her way back to her house, coming home from the maquiladora. The mural tells the story of Sagrario, and who she was. For example, when she disappeared she had a boyfriend. She gave her boyfriend a cage with two little birds, so that's why we painted those birds on the wall. Sagrario's family is from Durango— from the mountains, so we painted the mountains of Durango. She was in the choir at her church. She was also learning to play the guitar, so we painted a guitar. In the background we painted how Lomas de

FIGURE 4.4. Mural of Sagrario Gonzalez Flores. The mural is painted on the home of her Mother, Paula Flores, located in the colónia of Lomas de Poleo in Ciudad Juárez. Photo taken by author, Ciudad Juárez, 2016.

Poleo looks—where the house is located. We painted the mountains, and the trees, and all the vegetation we can see in the area. We also painted a sunset, which is very characteristic of Juárez—the colors—the yellow, the orange, the red. (L. Rocha, personal communication, June 20, 2016)

As in Maria Elena's mural, in addition to the mural symbols functioning to testifying to Sagrario's life, the painting and positioning of Sagrario's mural *on* her home is of significance. De Certeau's (1988) work speaks specifically about posthumous placement in relation to meaning: "Taking the dead . . . back to a symbolic place is connected to the labor aimed at *creating* in the present a place . . . something that must be *done*" (p. 101; emphasis added).

Levinas (1982) describes the "something to be done" in a stronger sense—as an order—or a command: "It [the face] orders me as one orders someone—one commands, as when one says: 'Someone's asking for you'" (p. 98). Thus, the haunting of the feminicidio victims' faces is inherently connected to the placement of the murals on a very particular object. Indeed, as José Luis points out, the location of the murals' matter matters:

> I think the murals are as important in our fight as the crosses—maybe more. Like the crosses, we have to think about where we put them [the murals]. We are here standing in the Alta Vista Preparatory School. We are painting the mural of a youth [Maria Elena] that has not been found yet. They [female students] might say, "Look, they are painting a mural of this girl"—and that's it, but I doubt it. Instead, I believe that they will look at the mural and wonder who she was—and they will realize that she was like them. The important part of these murals is that they serve as a prevention for the other girls. They will know that they either still haven't found her, or that no justice has been made. So, because of this, they will keep their guards up. (Personal communication, June 25, 2016)

Viewed through Levinas's proposition of the faces' commanding their audience's attention, and the strategic pairing of the murals with specific objects, the victims' haunting functions to command the girls to be vigilant and to always stay "on guard."

PROMULGATION

Extending Gordon's (2008) theorizing that haunting functions to make social violence known, I contend that coupled with the deployment of the victims' faces, haunting also functions to promulgate members of publics into action to address the social violence. As Levinas (1985) expounds: "Meeting the face is not of the order of pure and simple perception, of the intentionality which goes toward adequation. Positively, we will say that since the Other looks at me, I am responsible for him [sic], without even having taken on responsibilities in his regard; this responsibility is incumbent on me" (p. 96). In other words, the communities' responsibility to act has grown out of the physical encounters with the murals. Thus, while Gordon (2008) argues that forced disappearances by the state result in "producing ghosts to harrowingly haunt a population into submission" (p. 115), I suggest that this is not a predetermined outcome. Indeed, the faces' haunt in a counterhegemonic fashion, thereby not haunting a public into submission through making the reality of feminicidio known but rather, conversely, invoking an informed and politicized public equipped to act:

> I think that the mural project is very important here in Juárez. Until a couple of years ago, I mean people knew about the feminicidios, but only the symbol—the pink cross. People always talked about numbers: "there's so many missing girls, there's too much feminicidio," but there was something in the air—just in the air—like nobody really believed that reality. So, with the murals, we are giving that number a human form—a human shape. So, it is more difficult to ignore. Now people are *sure* that this happened, and the perception is different. I don't think that people now can keep saying the official position that they used to say—that it's a "dark myth." Now, that is more difficult to say, because they are seeing the murals everywhere. Even though you haven't seen them [the women] with your own eyes, you know them now—by their faces. The public thinks, "if a group of people including their moms are doing this, then it's real—the girls are real, and I need to do something." (Lluvia, personal communication, June 20, 2016; emphasis in original)

Thus, when people interact with the murals' faces, they are disabled from, to borrow Taylor's (1997) term, "percepticide": the perception that the feminicidio victims are not worthy of mattering, or that feminicidio is a myth, is disallowed (p. 119). Letty, Mother of Flor, explains:

> In my case, for Flor's mural, it's like asking for the government to see the reflection of the people who were victims, and that the government hasn't done anything. In my daughter's case, there are no suspects or anything. Through this mural I would like to tell the government to act. To find whoever is responsible. I want all the world to see that this is real. It is still happening. And these are not legends like the governor said. They exist. I want the world to know the truth. I want them to know that they left a scar for life, and that we need help. (L. Rivas, personal communication, June 28, 2016)

In addition to challenging "percepticide" about the girls and women's lives existing, people have *done* something. As Lluvia details:

> There has been a great variety of reactions to the mural project! I will begin at the local level. On the local level, the most important response was the involvement of the Mothers of the disappeared. Of course we would like to have 100 artists and a lot of funding to create tons of murals! But no, we are only two people, with very little funding. The Mothers wanted their daughters' murals to be painted *right away*, but we couldn't—we couldn't do all of the murals at the same time. These Mothers really owned this project—they organized themselves, and they provided their own funding. They also spoke to other urban artists and arranged for the painting of their own murals—various Mothers, like Sylvia Banda, Perla Loya, Anita Cueyar, Luz del Carmen, and Luz Elena—various Mothers. So they said, "Let's do this!" And they did it. For example, Anita Cueyar received funding from her local church and the neighborhood community members. Guys from that barrio painted her daughter, and many other girls who had disappeared—so, it was her organizing and heading-up everything. She told us: "You know what? I will do it myself." And we said, "Genius!" They now own the process that we feel we sparked. (Lluvia, personal communication, June 20, 2016; emphasis in original)

OBJECT-ORIENTED AFFECT

Although a dearth of scholarship theorizing affect, to date, analyzes its properties from its circulation between bodies and messages (e.g., Ahmed, 2010; Cvetkovich, 2012; McCann, 2016; Rand, 2015; Seigworth & Gregg, 2010; Tomlinson, 2010), recent work in new materialism asks us to consider the affective property of seeing, touching, and being with things themselves (e.g., Fleckenstein, 2016; Gries, 2016; Lacey, 2016; McNely, 2016). The "Faces of Feminicidio" project offers us a unique opportunity to consider the relationship between affect, objects, bodies, and publics. Maclovio, when discussing his role in the mural project, discusses the role of affect in the project's inception:

A mural depicting the victims of feminicidio would not be possible without the pain of all of these families. They are the primary element for this idea. I had never painted faces until I started to work closely with these families. They started transmitting the feeling of impotence and desperation, through my conversations with them [family members]. And like the Mothers would say: "I would rather be burying them than not know where they are—what they are doing to them, or what is going on." All of the Mothers' emotions—their pain—is what I am trying to transmit. (Personal communication, June 25, 2016)

As Lefebvre (1991) argues, "objects are real and therefore material in nature, but they are also symbolic, and hence freighted with affect" (p. 213). Situated in the barrios, amid all the violence in Ciudad Juárez, the murals elicit specific emotional responses from the victims' family members when they interact, materially, with what they commonly refer to as their daughters' "wall." In addition to the objects evoking cathartic affective responses from family members, as will be demonstrated, the residents in the neighborhoods feel that the mural faces function to protect them from the surrounding violence as their "guardians of the barrio."[4] Lluvia explains:

The "Guardians of the Barrio" was a phrase started by the neighbors of the Colónia de Esmezquital. When we finished the murals of Airis Estrella . . . and Ana Maria Gardena Villalobos, they started calling them [the girls] "The Guardians." These two girls were killed . . . I think that in this case, it's about the victims' ages, because they are girls— they were killed when they were very young. But feeling protected, I think, is also because of the traits of the barrio, and that particular *place* where the people live—it's a marginalized place, and there is a lack of many things there—like transportation and schools. So, the murals are more important for them, I think, because they don't have much—they are also very isolated there because it's [the neighborhood] far from the center of the city. They don't have access to basic services. So the mural is really *something* there, you know? (Personal communication, June 20, 2016; emphasis in original)

---

4. The "guardians of the barrio" faces of Airis Estrella and Ana Maria Gardena Villalobos are located in the neighborhood of Esmezquital in Ciudad Juárez.

Thus, *where* the object interacts with bodies is critical to suasive understandings. As Dickinson, Ott, and Aoki (2006) remind us: "Spaces of memory are better thought of as constitutive elements of landscapes . . . that . . . entail both physical and cognitive dimensions" (p. 30). The object's placement in the peoples' neighborhoods affords a suasive dimension. As one community member stated, "When I see them, I know that people care—that we are being watched over. They are guarding and protecting us—always with us" (L. Rivas, Mother of Flor Fabiola Ferrel Rivera, personal communication, September 18, 2016).[5] Thus, when people interact with the walls, affectively, the space is transformed from one of danger to one of safety.

Fleckenstein (2016) argues that objects, in their visual consumption, may "induce new perceptual habits and changed attitudes by blurring the boundaries between what one sees, how one sees, and who one might become as a result of that seeing" (p. 137). More specifically, McNely (2016) contends that when individuals traverse space and are confronted with the visual constitution of a thing, they are constitutive in their "affective affordances" (p. 143). Therefore, while community members living in the neighborhoods where the objects reside report feeling safe and protected, the Mothers also report a feeling of catharsis when interacting with the murals.

For example, when the Mothers aid in painting their daughters' faces—through each brushstroke, by touching the wall where their daughters' faces are painted—they feel emotionally and physically connected to them. Letty continues: "To me, it is cathartic, I feel that she is with me. She never leaves me." Irma, Mother to Marisela González Vargas, relayed, "Sometimes I just come here to sit next to her—to touch her—sometimes multiple times a day. I feel better knowing that she is with me" (I. Vargas, personal communication, June 21, 2016). Indeed, only through memorial "can the space of death be negated, transfigured into a living space which is an extension of the body" (Lefebvre, 1991, p. 221). Thus, object-oriented things give rise to affect not through a text but through the object's tactile properties—its *texture*. Maclovio recounts Marisela's children's relationship to her mural's wall:

---

5. Letty, who also lost her daughter Flor, was also the Godmother to one of the "guardians." After Maclovio and Lluvia painted her Goddaughter, she asked them to paint Flor.

The last mural we painted over the weekend was about Marisela Gonzalez Vargas. When she was murdered, she left behind four kids. But now they are older, and we see them say "there's my mommy!" The family told us that the kids cried at night because they thought that the mural portrait was beautiful, but that they would like to see her back with them—to *touch* her and *feel* her. But because they can't touch her, they touch her mural's wall. The family said that they cry less now. (Personal communication, June 25, 2016; emphasis in original)

Paula, because the mural covers her home's entire exterior, feels literally enveloped by her daughter: "She is in these four walls. I can touch and feel her with me. This is why my home contains her mural" (P. Flores, personal communication, June 25, 2016).

In these latter experiences, as these Mothers and family members describe, it is through the tactile relationship with the object itself that emotions such as safety, solace, catharsis, and comfort are materialized. So, while studies on affect, symbols, and bodies speak to the necessity of "affective capture" (McCann, 2016), I argue, instead, that the physical experiences between bodies and the objects themselves necessitate "affective *release*"—whereby visceral responses are produced and emancipated.

GOVERNMENT MURALS

To emphasize the significance of object-oriented affect in the haunting nature of victims' faces, I now juxtapose the "faces of feminicidio" project with the Mexican government's mural-painting project. Once the Mexican authorities realized the affective power of the family members' murals, the state attempted to co-opt the mural-making project. Maclovio explains:

So, after the murals we started, it became a big "thing." One guy from the government, belonging to one political party, took our political idea, and he started painting murals with the Mothers. And some of them accepted for their daughters to be painted by this official. This member of the government paid an artist to paint the faces of the girls in the downtown area. So, some of the Mothers started distancing

themselves from us. We saw right away his strategy of dividing the
movement. Rather than honoring the victims' lives, his idea was to
capture the images of some of the Mothers' daughters for his political
campaign—to have the Mothers on his side. I think he wanted to use
them . . . I think the way they used this situation was for their personal
interest and for political gain. I cannot use the face of Marisela and
make an exposition and sell it for thousands of dollars and not say
anything against the system. To be quiet is the same thing as doing
nothing. That's how they [the Mexican government] used them [the
Mothers], for politics. I think they used them for this past election. A
series of things occurred and this person's plan was out in the open—
it got exposed, and he was then forced to distance himself from the
Mothers—they had a falling-out once they figured out he was using
them. So, in the end, his plan was ruined. There were a couple of times
where the government's painted murals have also been damaged and
painted over—*they have no political weight, and that really is the point
of these murals.* (Personal communication, June 25, 2016; emphasis
added)

I posit that the murals have no "political weight" because the
government's murals do not haunt, or elicit an emotional response.
Instead, they act as empty referents and vacant signifiers. The state
murals, for example, are not based on interviews with the Mothers
about their daughters' embodied lives. As Maclovio reminds us:

It isn't really about painting the face of the young girl, but her story—
what she liked, or studied, or what she liked to eat. So, like this mural,
all the other murals we have painted have this theme. It is not about
just painting a beautiful portrait, but about her story—her *life.* Like
this one [Maria Elena], we painted an elephant because it was a gift for
her Mom . . . their lives are the essence of the painting. So it's about
that—their stories represent the lives that were ripped from them.
(Personal communication, June 25, 2016; emphasis in original)

The Mexican government murals are always produced ironically, or
perhaps not, in assembly-line fashion—a face and a rose, a face and a
rose. However, we know nothing of the face's *life*—the face's corporeal
history. Butler's (2004) work on the politics of mourning is useful in

this illustration. Butler (2004) contends that the public mourning of a corporeal subject is always a political process. Indeed, as documented in the preface, through the Mexican government's hegemonic tactic of articulating the feminicidio victims' bodies as those of prostitutes, drug mules, and/or gang members, bodies require discursive articulations in proving which bodies "qualify as grievable" (Butler, 2004, p. 32). Because the state's murals do not present a corporeal life—one of "corporeal vulnerability" (Butler, 2004, p. 16)—the objects function, literally, as just another face: not worthy of mourning and certainly not worthy of political intervention. The bodies' matter, through a lack of affect, does not promulgate, testify, or evoke cathartic release. The murals' matter effectively does not matter.[6]

CONCLUDING THOUGHTS

This chapter offers several contributions to the theoretical considerations on the role of affect and its relationship to objects. Importantly, as demonstrated, "object-oriented-affective" properties are only triggered via human mediation. And that human mediation entails discernment, the politics of representation, and speaking truth to power. Through the juxtaposition of the Mexican government's murals with the "Faces of Feminicidio," we see clearly that the affect emitted from the murals' properties is deeply foregrounded in the "behind the scenes" work that Maclovio and Lluvia painstakingly accomplish. What is important to remember is that the murals only "haunt" because they are representations of the women's and girls' material lives that no longer exist. The affect, while represented in the object, is rooted in the material—which preceded the object's existence. Further, the object's placement is of particular importance in relation to the affect that is conjured. As pointed out with the "Guardians of the Barrio" mural, the notion of safety is inherently connected to the barrio in that that is where the community members reside.

---

6. It is critical, here, to note that I am analyzing the government's symbolic strategies that exist in the victims' portrayals, and *not* the victims themselves. Additionally, Maclovio and Lluvia are discussing the importance of repainting the government murals, in concert with the victims' family members, to more fully represent the victims' lives.

Finally, although the "Faces of Femicide" is a visual rhetorical project, just like the lived history of the women's and girls' lives is always "there," the mural-as-object also cannot escape its neocapitalist rooting. For instance, always of particular concern with the mural project, according to Maclovio and Lluvia, is the question of sustainable capital. Walls crumble. Paint fades. Buildings are torn down. Other times, the wall that a Mother has chosen for her daughter to be painted on is sold, and the physical space becomes no longer available. Indeed, as of this writing the mural that I painted with Mac—that of Maria Elena— is in jeopardy, as the Alta Vista Preparatory School's funding may be cut, and the school may be shut down. Where, then, will Maria Elena's mural go? The precariousness of the capitalist undergirding is an ongoing concern that must be attended to, if haunting, as a viable rhetorical strategy, is to continue. Further, although some murals risk losing the power of their capital to endure, conversely, some of the objects also risk commodity fetishization.

For example, when interviewed, Paula Flores, Mother of Sagrario, indicated that on several occasions she has considered painting over Sagrario's mural on her home, because her home has become a "tourist attraction" rather than a physical, habituated space that affords comfort, safety, or even a call to activist action. Paula explains: "I feel like these walls have become a tourist attraction. People now come and just want to take pictures" (personal communication, June 25, 2016). For the time being, however, Paula has decided to leave the mural-as-object intact, as she does not want the government to feel that they "have won." Thus, questions of the affective power of objects must not be viewed as a priori, and must always be carefully attuned to questions of matter such as infrastructural support, as well as the real risk of the object lapsing into a form of commodity fetishization. Indeed, the fetishization of the mural-as-object is a dangerous result of the public viewing the murals through a gaze of wonder rather than through a critical gaze of political indignation. To fetishize the object of the dead women forestalls any calls to action.

CHAPTER 5

Lifeless or "Vibrant Matter"?

THIS CHAPTER interrogates the new materialist theoretical concept of *vibrant matter*. The concept stems from Bennett's (2007) version of new materialism that she defines as "vital materialism," which seeks to grant "vitality to nonhuman bodies, forces, and forms" (p. 122). Bennett (2007) discusses this agentic vitality of matter as "kicking back" at human agents. Bennett's (2009) project defines matter as "the materialities usually figured as inanimate objects, passive utilities, occasional interruptions or background context—figured, that is, in ways that give all the active, creative power *to humans*" (p. 92; emphasis in original). Her work looks at stem cells, fish oils, electricity, metal, and trash as exemplars of vibrant and agentic matter.

The claim that matter is inherently vibrant—consisting of inherent agentic properties—is perhaps the most intriguing premise of theorizing on new materialism in relation to the study of feminicidio. This is because one of the primary drivers of justice for the family members of the feminicidio victims are the feminicidio remains—the bones. Within the bones, of course, reside potentially agentic properties— DNA. Other things, however, also potentially function as "actants"— girls' and women's discarded clothing, jewelry, shoes, or handbags, for instance. For Bennett, the agency resides in the material property itself, not in the human use of said material. So, for example, electricity and stem cells, according to Bennett (2009), are "emergent properties" in and of themselves. The matter's agentic properties, according to Bennett (2009), are not predicated on their distribution or circulation or human mediation—rather, they are inherently powerful. To test this theoretical underpinning of vital materialism, I turn to the rastreos [searches] for the bones of the feminicidio victims to test their "vibrancy" in relation to the family members' project of recovery and identification of the feminicidio remains for justice. Before turning to an analysis of this theoretical claim, I first provide background on the rastreos for the feminicidio victims' bones and DNA.

ARROYO DEL NAVAJO

Currently, the Arroyo del Navajo, located in the remote outskirts of Ciudad Juárez, is commonly known as the "cemetery of women." In 2011 it was uncovered that the valley site was a dumping ground for Juárez feminicidio victims. As of this writing, the remains of 19 women have been discovered.[1] Although most of the victims' bodies were dumped during the fourth wave of violence, during the lost years of state militarization between 2008 and 2011, the use of the Arroyo del Navajo site as a dumping ground for bodies dates back to the late 1990s.

Susana, Mother of Maria, explains how even after the Inter-American Court of Human Rights decision, the murders continued in the Arroyo del Navajo:

---

1. The Arroyo del Navajo victims identified, as of this writing, are Idaly Juache Laguna, Maria Guadalupe Pérez Montes, Marisela Avila Hernandez, Yanira Fraire Jaquez, Brenda Berenice Castillo, Jessica Terrazas Ortega, Jessica Leticia Pena Garcia, Lizbeth Aviles Garcia, Virginia Elizabeth Dominguez, Andrea Guerrero Venzor, Deysi Ramirez Munoz, Beatriz Alejandra Hernandez Trejo, Perla Ivonne Aguirre Gonzalez, Jazmin Tailen Celis Murrillo, Monica Janeth Alanis Esparza, Lidia Ramos Mancha, Lilia Berenice Esquina Ortiz, and Esmeralda Castillo Rincón. A 19th victim remains unidentified. Although five men have been sentenced to a combined 697 years for the murders, because of inconsistencies, allegations of forced confessions, and continued doubts by family members, Santiago González, legal coordinator for the Mesa de Mujeres [Network of Women] reported, the Arroyo del Navajo feminicidio cases are "still open" ("Continued Open Investigations," 2016).

Since they [the court] made that ruling, the problems with the Arroyo del Navajo started. That's where my daughter was found. Unfortunately, they only found remains—and her whole body was not found. They first announced that they had found nine women, then 11. From 11 they [authorities] went to 16, and from 16 they [authorities] then said 19. What is going on?! What happened with what the Inter-American Court—with what they said? That's what I would like to know. Why do feminicidios continue to happen here in Juárez? My daughter was found there in the valley riverbed. The day they came to tell me that they had found my daughter, I had been desperately searching for her. They came and told me that they had found remains, and that among those remains were those of my daughter. (S. Rodriguez, personal communication, June 27, 2016)

Additionally, although in 2015 five men who were accused of abducting the women for forced prostitution and drug-dealing were sentenced to prison, the Mothers and family members have no confidence in the convictions because of the same judicial irregularities, falsehoods, and inconsistencies that marred the "cotton field" case ("Frontera NorteSur," 2016).

Arroyo del Navajo, where the mass graves exist, also has a clear connection to the production of capital. Maclovio explains the neoliberal capitalist history of the valley:

The Arroyo de Navajo also has a strong tie to the maquiladora sector. Once a rich valley for the harvest and production of cotton, it literally became a dead zone due to the building of the maquiladoras. Before NAFTA, the most fertile land was here in the Valley of Juárez. A lot of things were produced here. There were flowers and fruit trees. The best cotton in the world was produced in Egypt, and the Valley of Juárez. The valley was famous for cotton production, but it started to plummet when the wastewater from the maquiladoras seeped into the valley. And the Rio Bravo water belongs to the US, so they would have to authorize its use. What happened later to the valley is that the maquiladoras started to spring up. What was once fertile land was now used for these factories. The biggest maquiladora of Juárez is here in the valley. So, once production started in the factories, there was less demand for the products that were farmed in the valley, so more people were forced to move to the city. The only people who remain are the seniors. The youth left the valley because there were no jobs. So, that is what caused the death of the valley. Right now it is practically abandoned. After that, organized crime also started to situate themselves here. (Personal communication, June 25, 2016)

In other words, Juárez's largest cemetery became a dead zone because of globalization, long before victims' bodies were ever disposed of there. Arroyo del Navajo, once a rich, fertile site, was killed off by the maquiladoras' pollution and destruction of the land. Similarly, the other prominent Juárez site of mass dumping of bodies was also a formerly thriving cotton field—prior to the maquiladora association clearing the land and constructing their headquarters there. We must view space as "produced and reproduced in connection with the forces of production. And these forces, as they develop, are not taking over a pre-existing, empty or neutral space, or a space determined solely by geography, climate, anthropology, or some other comparable consideration" (Lefebvre, 1991, p. 77). Consequently, I argue that we must consider the family members' rastreos [searches] for their daughter's material remains in the context of spaces that were already "killing fields" for the neoliberal factories' modes of production.

Because there "can be no decontextualized generic body or matter, be it human or nonhuman, organic or inorganic" (Roy & Subramaniam, 2016, p. 28), this chapter analyzes the rastreos for the feminicidio remains in relation to the necro-/narcopolitics of the state. Material-discursive phenomena analyzed in this chapter include shovels, picks, whistles, gloves, plastic bags, clothing, bones, and DNA.

CITIZEN ACTION COMMITTEES

Because the Mexican government refused to conduct proper searches for the feminicidio remains, family members of the murdered and disappeared began forming "citizen action committees" to carry out searches for the bones of their missing family members.

On Friday, September 16, 2016, we joined a citizen action committee rastreo organized by Esmeralda's Father, José Luis. A femur bone, believed to belong to Esmeralda, had been previously recovered in the arroyo. The search party included members of eight different groups, composed of family members and activists, including Paso del Norte Human Rights Center, Grupo Vida, and Frenté Marginal. One search-party member explains the purpose of searching in this particular region of Ciudad Juárez:

> The objective was to search Arroyo del Navajo, a zone that since 2012 has been a dumping ground for the bodies and remains of women and men that have been reported as missing. Some remains belong to men, but unfortunately we don't have the statistics from the attorneys general's office for how many of these men have been reported missing. We know that there are 106 young women who are missing, according to el Colegio de la Frontera Norte. Unfortunately, it is also reported that about 500 men are missing as well. We are searching for those 606 missing people. We know that organized crime used this area as a dumping ground, and perhaps Mexican government authorities could be involved as well. This is one of our primary motivations for our search in Arroyo del Navajo. We did this rastreo during the 16th, 17th, and 18th of September. This type of search is one of many being carried out in this country. Unfortunately, there are many missing people. They might be missing because of organized crime, or their own state authorities took them. Searches have been carried out in Guerrero, Veracruz, Coahuila, and Torreon. We consider these searches successful. We have located or identified people who have been missing in the past, so we decided to carry out more of these searches here in Juárez. I want to stress that Arroyo del Navajo isn't the only place where you can find remains. This zone was picked because various remains of young girls and women have been found. So we are looking for these women. (Anonymous, personal communication, September 18, 2016)[2]

---

2. These searches are going on in every state of Mexico as part of a nationwide movement by family members and activists of the disappeared. There are over 30,000 missing people, dating back to cases in the 1970s. As a *Los Angeles Times* headline recently reported, "Mexico Is One Big Cemetery" (McDonnell, 2016).

ENACTING THE ROLE OF THE STATE

Because of the necro-/narcopolitics of the Mexican government, family members and activists must embody the role of the state and conduct the rastreos themselves. Oscar Viesca, Father of Silvia (Fanny), one of the disappeared, explains how the committees were formed in response to the Mexican government's ineptitude and negligence:

> In the beginning, they [authorities] did not help us one bit! The investigations, like many other cases, were carried out by us. They would ask us what we had or if we knew anything new. But this is supposed to be their jobs! It falls to the family members because we are the ones who feel it. We are the ones with the sense of urgency to find our lost ones. In our case, they didn't help us. We have about one year with this new governor and he is the first to make an effort, but it hasn't been sufficient. Nothing has been recovered for the Grupo Vida [Group for Life] or the other three groups from Coahuila. So the government has found nothing for any of the groups. I am speaking of people who have disappeared and have a file already, like my daughter. She will have been gone for 12 years, but they have no clue where she could be. The government just cannot do this job. It seems that they just don't want to. This is why we take it upon ourselves. This is why we have been doing this for 12 years and have been asking for help. But we haven't accomplished our goals. What we did yesterday is supposed to be the government's job. The local precincts are supposed to do these jobs in all of the states, but they don't do it! We are the ones finding bodies and remains. I don't know why the government isn't doing it. Maybe they are in collusion, inept, uninterested, or they just don't have the will to do it. (Personal communication, September 17, 2016)

Similarly, Rosa, Mother of one of the disappeared, echoes this frustration with the state:

> The government doesn't do anything! I would recommend that they do their jobs. A lot of this is their fault! If they had done their job in the first place, none of this would be happening. The only thing they do is take home a paycheck. That is the only thing they are doing. They are

FIGURE 5.1. Rastreo in Arroyo del Navajo. Day one of the search for remains in the Arroyo del Navajo [Riverbed of Navajo]. The bus transporting the family members could not make it over a ditch, so they were forced to walk in excess of one mile to get to the "home base" search site. The desert was very hot that day, and family members had to carry their own tools for digging, as well as rations such as water and food supplies. Photo taken by author, Ciudad Juárez, 2016.

sitting, doing nothing, and collecting their wages. They leave us without support, and it is not just! (R. Garcia, personal communication, September 17, 2016)

Indeed, as previously explicated, due to the logic of state necro-/narco-politics, some bodies are worthy of mourning, and others are not. The worth of the matter of bodies must be understood "as the effect of a dynamic of power, such that the matter of bodies will be indissociable from the regulatory norms that govern their materialization and the signification of those material effects" (Butler, 1993, p. xii).

In the instances where government officials did "search," the results were often, as documented in the preface, falsified or discarded altogether:

> When we went outside of the building, we came across Francisca Galvan, who is the founder of the Committee for Missing Girls in the City of Juárez. Francisca asked how long my daughter had been missing, and I told her over one year. She asked if I had gotten a genetic test taken yet, and I told her I didn't know what that was. She said, "A DNA test." I asked her why they would need that of me and she said, "I don't want to alarm you, but they have various unidentified bodies in the morgue that have been sitting there for years. They refuse to release the results. So, the DNA test could help identify those bodies." After that, I asked the authorities permission to see inside the box—to see if it was Cinthia. We thought what we saw was wrong. When I opened the government box, I found that they had presented me with a box filled with trash, instead of her bones. I broke down right there. I felt anger and rage, anxiousness and sadness. What I wanted was my daughter's bones. I don't know. It was surreal, and I started to cry. I thought, "I don't want to receive my daughter's remains like this. I don't want to see what I am seeing in this place." (K. Castañeda, personal communication, May 15, 2016)

RASTREO MATTERS

The family members and activists participating in the searches have no choice but to purchase their own tools and forensic equipment. To dig for remains and properly catalog the forensic evidence, family members transport objects such as shovels, picks, earth sticks ground poles, rope, whistles, gloves, tape, and resealable plastic bags. The objects are a necessity, as family members often face the task of collecting the bodies' matter:

> We, at Grupo Vida, carry out searches on Saturdays. We are located at an area where we found over 100 human remains. Some are very burned. The operation changes from area to area. In Baja California, for instance, they dissolved them [the bodies] with acid. In Coahuila,

they killed them, dismembered them, and took out their insides. They
then put them in barrels to burn them with fuel. They did this all
night, and in the morning they would break the barrels. So this is why
we have found many small burned fragments. So it is very difficult
to identify [remains]. Coahuila has interesting methods to help identify the bodies, so we learn from each other, but the whole country is
screwed! It is a mess—like an open faucet of bodies. (O. Viesca, personal communication, September 17, 2016)

Additionally, because the family members and search-party volunteers
possess no formal training to handle DNA matter, group members must
always rely on the informal training of other civilian action groups:

To enact this search, we counted on Grupo Vida. It is an organization that was founded many years ago in this country. They carry out
these types of searches. The government of Coahuila now helps them.
They were interviewed about three weeks ago in Coahuila. We asked
for their help, and thankfully, they were able to come. We needed to
know how to conduct our search—especially because the area we were
searching in spans 4,000 acres. So, with their experience, we were able
to properly go about this search. The search members were, as will be
discussed, successful in locating remains, but 95 percent of the arroyo
has yet to be searched, and things that were discovered led to new
unanswered questions from family members. We identified a natural well, for instance. It is important for authorities to search there.
Maybe there are objects or remains located there that are related to
some crimes. So it is important to search there. Of course, we thank
everyone here. We thank the organizations, activists, and especially
Grupo Vida from Torreon, Coahuila. We know that without your par-
ticipation, this search wouldn't be possible. We consider these searches
a success, especially because of the obstacles we faced from our own
state authorities. (Anonymous, personal communication, September
18, 2016)[3]

3. During the search for remains in the "Arroyo del Navajo" [Stream of Navajo],
we were constantly monitored by the Mexican military and federal police armed with
rifles and machine guns. These same authorities did not aid in the search for any

MAKING MATTER MATTER

Once the victims' matter is collected, the family members, activists, and civil society organizations hold public press conferences, using the modality of publicity, to circulate the findings to the wider public consciousness. Discursive strategies of persuasion must now attend to how the matter is taken up by external bodies and actors. As Rickert (2013) reminds us: "The thing matters to rhetoric insofar as rhetoric not only attends to things but . . . acknowledges that things are part of rhetoric's condition of possibility" (p. 208). One search-party member communicated our rastreo's findings to the wider public:

As all of you know, the 13th of September was the first press conference to inform every one of the searches that were going to take place. These searches were for women who have disappeared—men and women. Women are the focal point, but some organizations also have men in mind with these disappearances. These civil groups search for justice, truth, and for that truth to be known. The truth should be public. Everyone should know the steps taken in search of this truth to try and bring justice. The first human right is the right to life. (J. Monárrez-Fragoso, personal communication, September 17, 2016)

However, just because the family members have collected the matter, there is no guarantee that the state will have the matter tested.[4] Instead, the necropolitical state hegemony, as demonstrated, constrains "the domain of what is materializable" (Butler, 1993, p. 10). José Luis expounds his concern that the identification process will not be completed:

We hope that they [authorities] will finish processing the potential evidence. They processed 22 of them [bones]. What happened was that 19 of them were 100 percent human, according to the medics. The other four pieces of remains were perhaps from animals, or they couldn't identify them. But 19 were human. Some of them were pieces of cloth-

---

remains. At the end of the second day, our group was harassed in one perimeter of the desert, with the state asking what we were doing there and whose permission we had.

4. Family members used objects such as rocks, wood sticks, and red cloth to denote search boundaries and to mark evidence that was found.

FIGURE 5.2. Possible feminicidio remains. Image of remains thought to be human ribs. Because there was no proper forensic team provided by the state on day two of the search, the bones were marked with things such as rocks and a T-shirt, but there is no guarantee that the authorities will collect them and have the matter tested at the forensics laboratory. Over the two-day search, 42 items of physical remains and/or material evidence were found. Photo taken by author, Arroyo del Navajo, 2016.

ing with bloodstains. My companions took video and photos and recorded where they were found. I am more focused on the search, but the others have the documentation and need to make sure it gets processed so that we get our answers. (Personal communication, September 16, 2016)

As this chapter has demonstrated, the victims' remains of bones and DNA exemplify the importance of Bennett's (2005) argument that "nonhuman materialities [function] as actors" (p. 446). As the Mothers have stated repeatedly: "All I want is my daughter's remains. I want her with me." At the same time, although DNA "acts," by revealing the identity of the family members' missing daughters, even if the DNA is accepted into evidence by the state, as detailed, because of the ongoing necro-/narcopolitics of tainting, destroying, and falsifying evidence, the matters' ability to function as an *inherent* vibrant actor for justice is disrupted, and hence negated. José Luis elucidates this point:

The authorities say that there is no more evidence in the Arroyo del Navajo, but on the 16th of September, the first day of the searches, we found remains. We found more than a dozen pieces of clothing with bloodstains, so that makes us doubt them. The authorities have wanted to give us a bone for a single body. They just want to tell us that this is our daughter. We are doing these searches because this is where Esmeralda's bone supposedly was. We are going to get a definitive answer. The authorities just give you a bone and then they just want to close the case. (Personal communication, September 16, 2016)

The treatment of matter, I contend, always necessitates an interrogation of how the matter is mediated by ongoing external forces. In so doing, as Clare (2016) reminds us, "a new materialist understanding of politics need not find politics in the power relations between entities beyond the human but rather can turn to how power relations among humans entail more-than-human forces" (p. 68).

VIBRANT MATTER?

Upon conclusion of the three days of searches, the results were made public:

So what were the results? On the first day we found 42 remains, clues and evidence—a pink item of clothing with what appears to be blood and underwear. These 42 remains could belong to one person, or to many. This will have to be determined in the labs. Because of the decay present in these remains, we cannot identify if they belong to a male or a female. We believe that this is a first step for one or many families to recover their loved ones' remains. On September 17th we found 12 remains, including a shirt, and a woman's bag, at five different points. (Anonymous, personal communication, September 18, 2016)[5]

Here, I would like to return to Bennett's (2010) depiction of encountering matter as a process filled with "vibrancy" and "wonder." In my searching for lifeless matter alongside the family members, when con-

---

5. Bones found included remains from a spine, ribs, and a tibia (Nieto, 2016).

fronted with remains, family members used words such as "disgusted" and "horrified." José Luis' testimony exemplifies the problematics of Bennett's (2010) operationalized definition of matter:

We have demanded that the government search for our daughters. Even though we have hopes of finding them, we are conscious that they might very well be dead. We then become the ones responsible for searching for the remains. The people of Juárez help us. It takes a great toll to do this—both mentally and physically. But we have to do this because the authorities won't. They could provide some psychological help, because if we were to find remains of our loved ones, then it would affect us mentally. It is very difficult, but I have God that opens paths and peoples' hearts to move forward. (J. Luis, personal communication, September 17, 2016)[6]

Consequently, encountering matter necessitates a critical orientation—one rooted in an understanding of the matter's relationship to systems of power and logics of hegemony. There is no a-priori inherent property to matter—it is always influenced by larger structural forces. In addition to employing a critical framework when analyzing matter, we must also analyze the economic conditions in which the objects reside. So, while 42 pieces of remains were found, because of a lack of material resources only 4 percent of the Arroyo del Navajo valley could be traversed:

Approximately 80 people participated in these searches over the course of two days. The remains and clothing we found is a result of 10 hours of work. This was without much help from the state authorities. If we could find this amount of remains and objects in 10 hours, imagine if the authorities really applied themselves. We would be able to help a lot of families find their loved ones. Arroyo del Navajo has an open area of approximately 8,000 acres. We could only cover about 354 acres during these 10 hours—so only about 4 percent of the whole area. It is

---

6. José Luis stated that the findings included "only parts of the bone—chest, leg and shoulder and tailbone." Additionally, in an attempt to bypass suppression by the state, Señor Luis is looking for ways to publish the rastreo matter that is found online, so that the state cannot deny the evidence that the family members collect during the searches.

important to enhance these searches in order to cover this entire area! (Anonymous, personal communication, September 18, 2016)

In other words, one must ask, what does the matters' materiality involve? Pitts-Taylor (2016) contends that bodies are often shaped by structural and economic systems. She explains how bodies are not simply discursively constructed, without a situatedness but, rather, that their "organic parts[] and biological processes reconfigure themselves in intra-action with institutional forces, such as biocapitalism and securitization" (p. 9)—as is precisely the case with the feminicidio remains in Ciudad Juárez. In addition to capital constraints, necropolitical "security" predisposed family members' attempts to search for their loved ones' matter in several problematic ways. First, through the strategy of intimidation, the state attempted to stop the searches from being enacted:

The first obstacle was on the 14th of September. We were surprised that the state authorities carried out a "search" in the area we were scouting. This was surprising because they have never carried out a search in this zone. The state authorities said that these officers were attacked by a group of 20 gunmen, so they fled. We have to mention that our groups were also there in that zone for scouting and preparation. We were there at the same time this supposed attack took place. We were there for five hours and we didn't hear anything—no shots or anything. We didn't witness any attacks like the ones described by the authorities. We took photographs during this time. We were documenting everything, because we ran into the authorities four times during our scouting. (Anonymous, personal communication, September 18, 2016)

The second distinct suppression force of the state necro-/narcopolitics was evidenced through the strategy of intimidation:

They pointed their guns at us and made us get out of our cars, and asked many questions as to what we were doing. When they were able to identify one of the members of the search, they realized we were the activist group. They knew what we were doing there . . . they created a climate of terror for the search party.[7] Because of this climate, many people who had signed up to be a part of this search decided not to attend. We had about 100 people confirmed for this search and the numbers went down [on the second day] because of these incidents. (Anonymous, personal communication, September 18, 2016)

Regardless of these suppression strategies, family members have committed to continue ongoing monthly searches for their family members' remains. Family members and activists in Ciudad Juárez and Chihuahua will never stop searching for their loved ones' remains: "We must continue with these searches. The first three searches are just the beginning of many more to come" (J. Luis, personal communication, September 17, 2016).

CONCLUDING THOUGHTS

Thus, while the family members will continue conducting rastreos, this chapter's analysis has demonstrated the numerous problematics in the new materialist's theoretical positioning of matter's inherent nonmediated agentic properties. Although, scientifically speaking, the victims' inherent DNA properties can indeed function as actants for justice, this matter must *always* and *already* navigate terrains of power and hegemony. For example, the families continue to lack the monetary resources necessary to purchase the objects and tools needed to search and dig, in addition to covering the exorbitant travel costs. Further, even when the matter is recovered, as demonstrated, there is no guarantee that the state will properly catalog and test the victims' DNA properties. Also, as established, due to the ongoing harassment and lack of security measures instituted for the search-party members, and because the space where the vital matter resides is literally *controlled* by the cartels, it is extremely difficult for the family members and activists to inhabit the space where the matter resides to even access their loved one's matter. As Pink (2012) reminds us, "intra-action between suasive objects always operates within power-infused environments" (p. 48).

---

7. The entire time I was searching for remains, I was followed closely by military personnel pointing their machine guns in my face.

Thus, the bones' "vibrancy," as an *inherent* actant for justice, becomes, as demonstrated throughout these examples, a *subordinate* feature of the hegemonic forces of the necro-/narcopolitics of the state. The vibrancy is unable to be extracted. Any vibrant properties are active "only if there is an excess, an available surplus, superfluity and an actual expenditure thereof" (Lefebvre, 1991, p. 177). Ultimately, even when the remains are recovered and properly tested by the state, the matter still requires mediation: "The recovered bones must often be interceded by forensic specialists, as the bones' DNA is unable to be identified due to climate and carbonization of bone remains" (J. Herrera, personal communication, September 17, 2016).[8] Consequently, if the matter's actant "vibrancy" cannot be extracted and dispersed, it is a futile endeavor. The matter has no use value. "Vibrant matter" is rendered worthless. Thus, family members proceed in the searches for their family members' bones not with "vibrancy" or "wonder" but with fear and determination to counter the ongoing mediated hegemonic forces of the necro/narco corporate state that attempts to block their ongoing attempts in making their daughter's feminicidio's matter matter.

---

8. José (Angel) and I were in the same search group. He, as part of Grupo Vida, helped train us in how to properly handle any recovered physical material or remains.

CONCLUSION

THIS BOOK has been a delicate dance between moving theories of materiality in new directions and keeping true to my scholar-activist political commitments of embodying justice for and with the women of Juárez. Thus, I have an ethical and moral obligation not only to attempt to push theory in useful ways but to also offer concrete solutions for family members and activists who continue to work for justice on the ground in Ciudad Juárez and Chihuahua, Mexico. Thus, this book's conclusion first offers concrete suggestions for political change on the ground, in Ciudad Juárez, in attempts to stop the impunity surrounding these gendered crimes. Currently, this new, fourth wave of activists in Ciudad Juárez are engaging in ongoing justice projects pertaining to the border materialist issues of poverty, narco violence, government corruption, and neoliberalism in sophisticated attempts to enact structural change to halt the feminicidios in Juárez.

These activists are united in struggle, working side by side with the first-wave Mothers, and a new generation of family members and activists who are not only saying "!Ni Una Más!" [!Not One More!] but also rallying behind a new slogan, "Ni Una Menos!" [Not One Less!], which translates to "One Is Too Many!" "We Want Zero!" These current political projects, based on my research, must continue to work to address the following four specific categories in the ongoing attempts to prevent and end the Juárez feminicidios: legal structures, cultural discourses, activist strategies and tactics, and neoliberal economic reform.

LEGAL CATEGORIES

First, feminicidio must be recognized as a legal category in the state of Chihuahua. As a former mayoral candidate explains:

> Here in Chihuahua, legally, the term *feminicidio* is not part of the legal language. There are only two states where *feminicidio* is not a term inside their legal language—as a crime. Chihuahua and Merida, Yucatan. Ok? And here, that's the funny part, because that term began to get used here, in Juárez. It's a contradiction. Because in most of Mexico, these crimes are already referred to as *feminicidio*. But Chihuahua is resisting making *feminicidio* a legal term. For example, for this one feminicidio case to be able to go to court, legal means had to be found in order to put it through. That's why they classified it as human trafficking and aggravated homicide, since they are the only legal terms that exist. But that is wrong. It is shocking. (V. Caraveo, personal communication, June 28, 2016)

In November 2016, as part of the International Day for the Eradication of Violence against Women, the governor of Chihuahua, Javier Corral Jurado, pledged to put forth an initiative that would indeed make the crime of feminicidio legally recognized in the state of Chihuahua. Jurado also appointed Paola Chávez Villanueva as the new head of the Specialized Prosecutor's Office for Women Victims of Crime for Gender Reasons. Jurado instructed Villanueva, as a first order of business, to reopen the abandoned cases of the disappeared and murdered women and pledged full compliance with the Inter-American Court of Human Rights' "cotton field" ruling, stating:

> I know that for seven years many of the resolutions have been violated since they have to do with the standardization of protocols such as training, building databases of victims, of training public ministries,

of reparation of the damage, and of effective investigations and indications that the own relatives have given. (As quoted in Prado, 2016)

Thus far, however, none of Jurado's promises have been implemented. Additionally, most of the Mothers of the victims and disappeared either boycotted the event or were present holding bright-pink protest signs reading "Stop the Indifference" and "¡Ni Una Más!" Juárez journalists referred to Jurado's speech as "a show," "a stunt," and a "political circus performance."

In addition to formally recognizing feminicidio as a legal category, Victoria Caraveo contends, the current rape laws must also change if other forms of gendered violence are to decrease:

If you are raped in Juárez, you have to prove to the judge that you were dressed correctly—that you were not provoking the subject who raped you. And then he is out of jail by paying 5,000 pesos—like 400 dollars. Then, he only needs to come back every 15 days—he has to come back to sign a book; that's all. (Personal communication, June 28, 2016)

Further, although Mexico has a population of roughly 60 million women, only 8.23 million women currently reside in one of the 41 municipalities where the Alba Protocol—a mechanism intended to combat violence against women through various gender alerts—remains active ("Gender Alert," 2016).[1] Other Mexican states and municipalities must follow suit.

Next, the collusion between organized crime and the state must be disarticulated:

Unfortunately, this abominable fact of feminicidio has extended throughout the whole country. You can see what is happening in Mexico City. Each day there are cases of assassinations and rape of women, and kidnapping of youth. So this is a very grave situation caused by negligence—and because it is clear that this is a state that protects

---

1. The eight Mexican states that have implemented some measure of the Alba Protocol are Campeche, Chihuahua, Colima, Distrito Federal, Morelos, Oaxaca, Sinaloa, and Veracruz. Since 2012, however, numerous activist organizations have demanded that gender alerts also be implemented in the states of Colima, Baja California, Sonora, Veracruz, Querétaro, San Luis Potosí, Nuevo León, and Chiapas ("Gender Alert," 2016).

narco-trafficking, organized crime, and criminals like the Zetas that are formed from our very own Mexican army. The fight against impunity continues and will keep existing. The people won't be silenced. The fight continues. (J. Galarza, personal communication, 2016)[2]

Because of this widespread collusion between the cartels and the Mexican government, it is imperative that an external forensic body be allowed permanent state residency:

> I ask myself, why, if they are well-educated people . . . do they not use their resources and brains to get *outside* specialists to come in and investigate these crimes—not to just get an investigation specialist—no, no, no—not just that—to bring a helicopter—a geographical expert, an anthropologist—to analyze the area where they [victims] were found. To this day, they haven't done that, and they say they can't. (S. Rodriguez, personal communication, June 27, 2016; emphasis in original)

In addition to feminicidio not being recognized as a legal category, activists belonging to human rights and civil society organizations, as well as family members of the victims, contend that even if this legal remedy is attended to, it does nothing to address the thousands of continued forced disappearances (Díaz, 2016). In August 2016, because of activist pressure on this issue, the governor of Chihuahua, Javier Corral Jurado, after meeting with the civil associations of Cosyddhac, Justicia Para Nuestras Hijas [Justice for our Daughters], and the Center for Women's Rights, announced that he would be creating a specialized

---

2. Judith is one of the original first-wave activists. She hopes to return to Juárez soon: "I left Juárez in 1998. I first went to the federal district because I became president of the Comite Nacional Independiente Pro-Defensa de Presos, Perseguidos, Detenidos Desaparecidos y Exiliados por Motivos Politicos (CNI). When I became president of CNI, we imposed some changes. One of these changes was the name. We modified it to Asociación de Familiares de Detenidos Desaparecidos y Victims de violaciones los derechos humanos (AFADEM). After becoming president of AFADEM, I then became Executive Secretary of FEDEFAM in 1999 in the 15th Congress. This was in Mar de Plata, Argentina, and I had to come live in Caracas, Venezuela, because this is where it was located. This is still a great experience of struggles and learning. I hope to return to my country [Mexico] soon. My organization has asked me to return."

prosecutor's office as part of the investigation of human rights violations and forced disappearances.

Jurado stated: "I will accompany them [family members]. We are going to open the doors. We will listen to them. We will review the [feminicidio and disappeared] cases and we will investigate, so that the families can meet their loved ones and know exactly where they are" (quoted in "Corral to Create," 2016). The efficacy of this new office remains to be seen. So although the victims' family members and activists remain skeptical, Irma González, former director of the Juárez Institute for Women, remains hopeful that with the instillation of the new National Action Party (PAN) government, family members' demands will finally be addressed:

> For six years these topics on women were delayed. There was persecution by the state government on these movements, and on the topics on women. They put a stop to many of our initiatives, including in the theme of legislation—not just on feminicidio but also on domestic and family violence, and on civil and political codes and penalties. Our state congress was mainly run by the Institutional Revolutionary Party (PRI), which was the same as the governor—so there was a strong block and critique—including much violence against the movement of women. This is why, for many social organizations, the change of government has been a means of hope—hope that we will finally be able to push these new policies forward. We believe that in October, when the new government and new governor step in, there will be very strong changes. But we must look at what is still legally absent in the state of Chihuahua. (I. Vargas, personal communication, June 21, 2016)

CULTURAL GENDERED NORMS

In addition to struggling for new legal language, laws, and precedents, dominant cultural norms pertaining to gender must continue to be challenged:

> If I am found dead—raped—why would it be? Because I'm pretty? Because I'm a woman? Because I'm young? Because I was in the wrong place—maybe wearing a skirt? Because some guy liked my tits and

he was like "Oh, I'm going to take that woman!" And I have been approached by men here in Juárez telling me, "I want to take you out." And I have said "No, thank you—no. I am very flattered, but I don't want to." They have said: "You are going to go out with me, and I'm not even asking you—you are going to do it, or I'm going to rape you, and kill you." Men feel so powerful, and they feel they have a right to tell you those kinds of things. And is the government even going to listen to you? No. Why do we get raped? I was just telling this to a guy the other day: "If I find myself with five men in a room, they are going to rape me for sure—if they want to—for sure—they are going to rape me." And nobody talks about that in Juárez. Everyone remains quiet about it. In Mexico, we are living that in the whole republic. In Juárez, in particular, it's a bloodbath for women, but nobody wants to talk about it. (J. Blanco, personal communication, June 28, 2016)

Professor Pérez believes that in Juárez, there has been a "feminicidio" movement but not a national "feminist" movement. Pérez believes that these current fourth-wave activist groups are beginning to tackle this deficiency more specifically but that more cultural and educational work needs to continue in this area (personal communication, June 27, 2016).

José Luis agrees with Professor Pérez, and is speaking out to other men regarding the rejection of dominant patriarchal gender roles and hypermasculinity in Ciudad Juárez:

Well, look, it is because we are in Mexico. In Mexico, men carry ancestral cultures. When I would fall down as a kid my father would tell me, "You better not cry. You have to keep it in. You are the one in charge of bringing home money. You are the one who rules. No one should see you cry. Hold that pain in." So I have learned—but I assure you that all of the fathers of the disappeared are crying alone at night. Their appetite also has gone away. They also suffer like the Mothers. We have the example of Don Juan. His daughter disappeared in 2011. He kept the sorrow inside. He didn't go out. He was depressed. After two years he died from that depression. So it is very important to make those calls to men to try and change that culture. We don't have to wake up in the morning and put on our mask of bravery. (J. Luis, personal communication, June 21, 2016)

LOCAL AND INTERNATIONAL PRESSURE

International pressure, to hold Mexico accountable for these gendered crimes, must continue:

> I asked the president of the International Court: "What can we do if the sentence was given about seven years ago, and only the monument and some money was given to the family, but other than that, nothing has been done?" His response was: "Only pressure. Keep pressuring them. We cannot make them go to prison because it is only a diplomatic solution—and they don't care about diplomacy. Pressure." (V. Caraveo, personal communication, June 28, 2016)

Local activism, as well, must continue to organize and exert pressure for change. A key component of this grassroots organizing, from the perspective of Lluvia, founding member of Frenté Marginal, is that it is crucial that activists not be co-opted by the state. Recently, however, an umbrella group, Red Mesa de Mujéres [Board Network of Women], which consists of 13 groups, formed a pact with the newly elected mayor, Armando Cabada. The pact includes government leasing of a new office building and a budget increase for the Municipal Institute for Women from 3 to 10 million pesos (Luján, 2016). During the "pact" press conference, the mayor stated:

> I knew that these organizations would come to an agreement . . . we have asked the three levels of government to attend to this problem of violence . . . we will work on issues through various independent methods. We have finalized our cabinet, and this cabinet will work cohesively where they will have periodic meetings so that we are all on the same page. We must earn our places and work for them. Both government and organizations will work together. And I am sure we will achieve our goals. I hope we all work together with great communication and in a cohesive manner. . . . let me add to this: if we can work

together, then our resources will be more effective. The budget is very limited, and we need to be creative . . . many things from public security, community centers and many things that help society. Resources are very limited. If everyone understands that—they have to carry their weight, then our resources will last. (Quoted in Luján, 2016)

Many activists, understandably, perceive this rhetoric as the same failed discourse that has stemmed from the state since the feminicidios began—lies, failed promises, and more corruption. Lluvia points out her concern:

Recently, some grassroots groups, among them Network of Women, entered into the payroll of the municipal government of the corrupt Armando Cabada. In fact, Verónica Corchado, group member, is now the director of the Municipal Institute of Women. The problem is that this group now receives state funding—so now they become a kind of political buffer—whose main function is to mediate the organized, independent, and radical popular response. And this has been its function since the 1990s here in Ciudad Juárez. From there, the state is able to generate strategies to bust social movements. (L. Rocha, personal communication, June 20, 2016)

Another prominent activist and professor, Julián Contreras, points out: "You cannot put your faith in the same people who are the ones who have decimated—and who continue to kill your people" (personal communication, June 20, 2016). José Luis agrees with engaging in tactics for change that are grassroots in nature and that exist outside of state parameters. For instance, recently, José Luis authored an educational text, in the form of a comic book, about the forced disappearances and feminicidios happening in Ciudad Juárez, in order to reach young audiences:

We have been in approximately two preparatory schools, eight high schools, and six primary schools. We will also start to go into the community centers. These centers host young women from 14 to 16 years of age who are pregnant or don't have the opportunity to go to school, but need these materials and need to learn. We don't want them to be easy targets in this city. We managed to create three stories. We were able to put these [comic books] in public transportation [spaces] where many girls board them [buses] to go to the center of the city. We have placed them at the Benito Juárez Monument, where they [women and girls] also disappear. We have put them in a restaurant where we have identified the women being taken to. We have described how they are captured, how they are trafficked, and how they finally take their lives. Sometimes, they kill them [women and girls] without intention. Sometimes they just go overboard—and because they are mostly people who have a lot of economic power, they just send them to be buried at Arroyo del Navajo—or any other desert. All the stories in the comic books are real, but we only changed the names. Here [*pointing to the book*] we show how they are taken to Tijuana and how they are sold and exploited. We also placed photos of some of the girls that have been taken with the hopes of finding some of them. So this is what we give out after we speak to the young women. When we go to a primary school we give them a "cube," because they are younger. They have a different reading capacity, so we explain more things to them. So we give this to them, and we make a game for them to make a giant cube. (J. Luis, personal communication, June 21, 2016)

In addition to grassroots forms of education and community outreach, activists and family members also stress the necessity to organize around class-based forms of oppression in relation to the phenomenon of feminicidio.

NEOLIBERAL CHANGE

Although this book, in chapter 4 most specifically, has demonstrated how the "faces of feminicidio" victims, through their tactile and affective properties, have haunted publics into activism, Gordon (2008) also suggests that strategies of haunting may be constitutive of larger structural impact—of "something more" (p. 206). That "something more" is neoliberalism. Gordon explains: "Because ultimately haunting is about how to transform a shadow of a life into an undiminished life . . . this [is] necessarily [a] collective undertaking" (p. 208). Thus, while the rhetorical strategy of haunting is accomplishing its goal in Juárez of making lives matter, I contend that, ultimately, haunting should not simply be about transforming the memories of women's lives but about transforming the *system itself*. Thus, I extend Gordon's (2008) work by calling for a more radical strategy of mere haunting—that of an *exorcism* of capitalism itself. A move from a tactic of haunting to a strategy of exorcism necessitates that specific *structural*, not just individual, changes must occur.

As a former labor organizer and current activist details, this radical exorcism of neoliberal logics is currently underway:

> I think that a central objective continues to prevail for the workers, their livelihoods . . . obtaining better wages. In fact, last year, numerous workers began demonstrations—and after almost 10 years of not generating organizational processes within the maquiladoras, last year, in 2015, in six different companies, employees began to raise wages in order to improve their working conditions. So, right now, mainly is the goal to fight for better salaries—they are demanding a wage increase. What was achieved at the end of 2015 and the beginning of 2016 is that an independent trade union was registered—the first in the entire existence of the maquiladora industry here in Juárez. (V. Leyva, personal communication, June 27, 2016)

This union is now part of the Commscope maquiladora, formerly known as the ADC Factory, which produces fiber optics for Verizon, AT&T, Nortel, Telmex, and Televisa. On February 7, 2016, more than 150 workers held their first independent union meeting in over 30 years. At the meeting, the workers formally articulated their next goal: to press for a wage increase of 285 pesos per day, which translates to roughly $15.62 ("Maquiladora Workers," 2016).

In addition to a radical ideological shift in consciousness among the rank-and-file workers, more significantly, a fracture in the capitalist system itself is taking form. Professor Pérez explains:

> There is disenchantment among workers . . . and the lives of workers in the maquiladoras began to transform when workers left to find better conditions elsewhere. For example, workers came mostly from Veracruz with their whole families. They returned after realizing that they couldn't improve their way of life in Juárez. Other workers realized that they could earn income without needing to work in the maquiladoras.

Now, as well, the US has competition from other countries, including Mexico; the maquiladora industry keeps on growing, yet there are fewer people who want to work for maquiladoras. So, maquiladoras now employ all workers, regardless of whether they are male or female, as long as they meet the production needs that are required. In reality, this has a lot to do with the economic crisis—maquiladoras close and reopen again, some leave and new ones come. This has affected the job security of the maquiladoras and their employees, but has also resulted in a rejection of this type of economic system. (F. Pérez, personal communication, June 27, 2016)

Because of this capitalist crisis, Carrera (2016) argues, a restructuring of the neoliberal economy in Juárez is "more than a simple desire, it is urgent." Real structural reform must be brought about. In addition to the rejection of exploitative factory labor, the pillars of the narco state must also be overthrown. As Jorge, a member of la Línea/Juárez cartel, explained:

This is [selling drugs] like a normal business, like selling hamburgers. In this work, it completes families—the mother, the father, the children, the granny. There is no work [in Juárez], no matter how hard you study—there is no work . . . even if you study for a graduate or doctorate, what is the good if there is no work? A maquiladora pays 100 pesos a day for eight hours. Sometimes I think of my two girls, my wife, but no way. It's the only way to survive here, there is no work. (Quoted in Prado, 2016)

As demonstrated in chapter 1, the production of grassroots alternative economies, such as Las Hormiga's ecological toilets, functions as viable alternatives to the dominant necro/narco corporate system that currently dictates and governs peoples' lives within this border town. These themes, taken together, exemplify the challenges that fourth-wave activists must continue to attend to if the border materialism of Ciudad Juárez is to be radically transformed. As such, my research offers concrete foci for the political work that must endure on the ground in Ciudad Juárez during this fourth wave, in a world that is continually plagued by the devastating effects of neoliberal globalization.

NEW THEORETICAL DIRECTIONS

In addition to offering concrete suggestions for combating feminicidio on the ground through a hands-on engagement with the material properties that produce the feminicidios in Ciudad Juárez, this book proposes that the new materialist's decontextualization of matter, through its disavowal of the mediated properties of rhetoric and human agency, in conjunction with its lack of attention to the hegemonic and neoliberal forces that interact with said matter, has resulted in a theoretical problematic that is not just *post*human but *anti*human in its application. As Clare (2016) argues: "To the extent that new materialisms does not address the historical locatedness of its representations of materiality, its implicit critique of the subject may, in fact, inaugurate one" (p. 67). The phenomenon of the feminicidio in Ciudad Juárez must be examined through its neoliberal historical situatedness on the US–Mexico border. The killings and forced disappearances of the women and girls in Ciudad Juárez cannot be divorced from their historical and current political, cultural, and economic conditions.

Currently, in this historical moment—a moment when the lives of the women of Juárez do not matter in the context of society under neoliberal capitalism—we cannot afford to adopt the new materialist posthumanistic turn. I contend that this turn would have devastating consequences for future critical rhetorical projects and political endeavors. Ironically, Barad (2007) suggests that one of the most important tenets of new materialist work is the promise it holds regarding change and the hope for a better world. As this is a driving premise of new materialist research, it is incumbent, then, upon scholars engaging in new materialist work to demonstrate exactly *how* this is accomplished. Bennett (2009), when discussing her centering of "wonder" and "enchantment" as tropes that may yield a more ethical future, admits that a theoretical corrective may be in order:

> The promiscuity of affect means that it will *also* be unfaithful to any ethical re-deployment of it. I should have thought more about how to cope with or compensate for that fact, and because I didn't, it sounded easier than it is to transform commodity enchantment into non-commercial or counterhegemonic modes of activity. (p. 103; emphasis in original)

Indeed, as current rhetorical projects attempt to call attention to and engage in political projects to end the impunity surrounding the global phenomenon of feminicidio, this work must continue its focus on counterhegemonic modes of activity. The question then becomes what theoretical tools help us best accomplish this task. As I stated in the introduction, the new materialist scholarship's foci concerning questions of matter, objects, and the assemblage of things is integral to thinking through what role these material elements play in relation to the ongoing feminicidios in the free-trade zones of Ciudad Juárez. However, as my research has demonstrated, a turn to the material that disperses agency across everything and everywhere, and hence nowhere, in conjunction with muted human agency and a dismissal of the role of the root economic causes of the perilous conditions of the women of Juárez, only leads us further away from justice. This is not a road that as a critical scholar-activist I am willing to go down. Lives matter. The women of Juárez's lives matter.

Thus, this book has offered a theoretical corrective in its push towards new directions in rhetoric and materiality studies. Border materialism, as a theoretical frame, affords scholars not only the capacity to interrogate the victims' family members' and activists' counterhegemonic activities, but also a mechanism to analyze the material elements that work to produce, sustain, and perpetuate feminicidio. Border materialism, as a transborder perspective, has answered the call within the discursive shift of "feminicidio" to provide a theoretical framework that examines bodies and the material in relation to all of their social, cultural, political, and economic configurations.

Throughout this book, I have attempted to address the primary tenets of new materialist concepts informed by a new border materialism sensibility, in order to expose the new materialist theoretical limitations in their current various iterations. As the writing of a scholar-activist who does the public work of rhetoric in "the field," each chapter in this book has functioned as an important case study that tests the new materialist guiding principles through their application of them in relation to the on-the-ground counterhegemonic activist work and political projects in Ciudad Juárez and Chihuahua, Mexico.

Though my scholarship's applied work, in taking up the material concepts of the "re-assemblage of things," "matter-memory-making," "practiced matter," "object-oriented affect," and "making matter matter," informed by border materialism's keen eye for *how* these concepts operate in very specific historical, political, cultural, and economic contexts, I have provided tangible examples for how political projects that attend to the material may be accomplished. These theoretical concepts have presented new understandings not only of the material elements that function to produce feminicidios but also of how these same material objects, when mediated through human agency, have the potential to be rearticulated, repurposed, and reappropriated into projects for efficacious political change.

As this book has offered original insights into the relationship between the production of material things and feminicidios squarely rooted in a neoliberal context, I hope that it offers scholars studying the feminicidios—and similar ongoing devastating effects of globalization—new theoretical tools and insights to build upon. New directions in rhetoric and materiality must continue to confront these injustices in theory and praxis. !Ni Una Más!

BIBLIOGRAPHY

Achille, M. (2003). Necropolitics. *Public Culture,* 15(1), 11–40.

Ackerman, J. M., & Coogan, D. J. (Eds.). (2010). *The public work of rhetoric: Citizen-scholars and civic engagement.* Columbia, SC: University of South Carolina Press.

Aden, R. C. (2012). When memories and discourses collide: The president's house and places of public memory. *Communication Monographs,* 79(1), 72–92.

Agamben, G. (2005). *State of exception.* Chicago, IL: University of Chicago Press.

Agosín, M. (2006). *Secrets in the sand: The young women of Ciudad Juárez.* Buffalo, NY: White Pine Press.

Aguayo, A. J., & Hivoltze-Jimenez, A. (Prod./Dir.). (2010). *Ni una mas / Not one more* [Documentary]. Available from Vimeo. Retrieved from https://vimeo.com/41520366

Ahmed, S. (2010). *The promise of happiness.* Durham, NC: Duke University Press.

Ainslie, R. C. (2013). *Life in the heart of Mexico's drug war: The fight to save Juárez.* Austin, TX: University of Texas Press.

Alaimo, S. & Hekman, S. (Eds.). (2008). *Material feminisms.* Bloomington, IN: Indiana University Press.

Alcoff, L. M. (1995). The problem of speaking for others. In J. Roof & R. Wiegman (Eds.), *Who can speak? Authority and critical identity* (pp. 97–119). Urbana, IL: University of Illinois Press.

Althusser, L. (1971). Ideology and ideological state apparatuses. In L. Althusser (Ed.), *Lenin and philosophy and other essays.* New York: Monthly Review Press.

Amos, T. (1999). Juárez. *To Venus and Back* [CD]. Cornwall, UK: Atlantic Records.

Amnesty International. (2003). *Intolerable killings: Ten years of abductions and murders in Ciudad Juárez and Chihuahua.* Retrieved from http://www.amnestyusa. org/countries/mexico/document

Anderson, B. (2014). The forensic dentist who's reviving Mexico's unidentified corpses (NSFW). *Motherboard,* August 18. Retrieved from https://motherboard.vice.com/ en_us/article/still-life

Anzaldúa, G. (3rd Ed.). (2007). *Borderlands/la frontera: The new Mestiza.* San Francisco: Aunt Lute.

Arriola, E. R. (2010). Accountability for murder in the maquiladoras: Linking corporate indifference to gender violence at the U.S.-Mexico border. In Gaspar de Alba & Guzmán (Eds.), *Making a KILLING* (pp. 25–62).

Bacon, D. (2015). The maquiladora workers of Juárez find their voice. *The Nation,* November 20. Retrieved from https://www.thenation.com/article/ the-maquiladora-workers-of-juarez-find-their-voice/

———. (2016). Voices from the Juárez workers' movement. *NACLA,* April 6. Retrieved from http://nacla.org/news/2016/04/06/voices-ju%C3%A1rez-workers-movement

Barad, K. (1998). Getting real: Technoscientific practices and the materialization of reality *differences: A Journal of Feminist Cultural Studies, 10*(2), 87–128.

———. (2003). Posthumanist performativity: Toward an understanding of how matter comes to matter. *Signs, 28*(3), 801–831.

———. (2007). *Meeting the universe halfway.* Durham, NC: Duke University Press.

———. (2008). Posthumanist performativity: Toward an understanding of how matter comes to matter. In S. Alaimo & S. Heckman (Eds.), *Material feminisms* (pp. 120–156). Bloomington, IN: Indiana University Press.

Barla, J. (2016). Technologies of failure, bodies of resistance: Science, technology, and the mechanics of materializing marked bodies. In Pitts-Taylor (Ed.), *Mattering: Feminism, science and materialism* (pp. 159–172).

Barnett, J. T. (2015). Toxic portraits: Resisting multiple invisibilities in the environmental justice movement. *Quarterly Journal of Speech, 101*(2), 405–425.

Barnett, S., & C. Boyle (Eds.). (2016). *Rhetoric, through everyday things.* Tuscaloosa, AL: University of Alabama Press.

Barrera, G. (Prod.), & Nava, G. (Dir.). (2006). *Bordertown* [Motion picture]. Mexico: Möbius Entertainment.

Barthes, R. (1972). *Mythologies.* New York: Hill and Wang.

Bejarano, C. (2013). Memory of struggle in Ciudad Juárez: Mother's resistance and transborder activism in the case of Campo Algodonero. *Aztlán: A Journal of Chicano Studies, 38*(1), 189–203.

Bejarano, C. L. (2002). Las super madres de Latino America: Transforming Motherhood by challenging violence in Mexico, Argentina, and El Salvador. *Frontiers, 23*(1), 126–150.

Bennett, J. (2005). The agency of assemblages and the North American blackout. *Public Culture, 17*(3), 445–466.

———. (2009). Thing-power and an ecological sublime. In L. White & C. Pajaczkowska (Eds.). *The sublime now* (pp. 24–35). Newcastle, UK. Cambridge Scholars.

———. (2010). *Vibrant matter.* Durham, NC: Duke University Press.

———. (2015). Ontology, sensibility and action. *Contemporary Political Theory, 14*(1), 63–89.

Berndt, C. (2013). Assembling market b/orders: Violence, dispossession, and economic development in Ciudad Juárez, Mexico. *Environment and Planning, 45,* 2646–2662.

Biesecker, B. A. (2002). Remembering World War II: The rhetoric and politics of national commemoration of the turn of the 21st century. *Quarterly Journal of Speech, 88*(4), 393–409.

Biesecker, B. A., & Lucaites, J. L. (2009). Introduction. In B. A. Biesecker & J. L. Lucaites (Eds.), *Rhetoric, materiality and politics* (pp. 1–16). New York, NY: Peter Lang.

Blair, C., Jeppeson, M. S., & Pucci, E., Jr. (1991) Public memorializing in postmodernity: The Vietnam veteran's memorial as prototype. *Quarterly Journal of Speech, 11,* 263–288.

Blair, C., Dickinson, G., & Ott, B. L. (2010). Introduction: Rhetoric/memory/place. In G. Dickinson, C. Blair, & B. L. Ott (Eds.), *Places of public memory: The rhetoric of museums and memorials* (pp. 1–56). Tuscaloosa, AL: University of Alabama Press.

Blancas, P. R. (2010). We never thought it would happen to us: Approaches to the study of subjectivities of the Mothers of the murdered women in Ciudad Juárez. In Domínguez-Ruvalcaba & Corona (Eds.), *Gender violence at the U.S.–Mexico border* (pp. 35–59).

Blanco, L. (2009). The impact of reform to the criminal justice system in Mexico. *RAND Center for Latin American Social Policy.* Retrieved from http://www.rand. org/labor/centers/clasp/research/projects/mexican-criminal-justice-reform.html

Bonasso, S. (2012). *Juárez: A novel.* Los Gatos, CA: Smashwords. Author.

Bost, M., & Greene, R. W. (2011). Affirming rhetorical materialism: Enfolding the virtual and the actual. *Western Journal of Communication, 74*(4), 440–444.

Bowden, C. (1998). *Juárez: The laboratory of our future.* New York, NY: Aperture.

———. (2010a). *Dreamland.* Austin, TX: University of Texas Press.

———. (2010b). *Murder city: Ciudad Juárez and the global economy's new killing fields.* New York, NY: Nation Books.

Bowers, J. W., Ochs, D. V., Jensen, R. J., & Schultz, D. P. (2010). *The rhetoric of agitation and control* (3rd ed.). Long Grove, IL: Waveland.

Braidotti, R. (2010). On putting the active back into activism. *New Formations, 68*(16), 42–57.

Bryant, L. R. (2011). *The democracy of objects.* Ann Arbor, MI: Open Humanities.

Bueno-Hansen, P. (2010). *Feminicidio*: Making the most of an "empowered term." In Fregoso & Bejarano (Eds.), *Terrorizing women* (pp. 290–311).

Butler, J. (1993). *Bodies that matter: On the discursive limits of "sex."* London: Routledge.

———. (2004). *Precarious life: The powers of mourning and violence.* London: Verso.

Cabada, A. (2016, June 19). Juárez mayor-elect vows transparency. *El Paso Times.* Retrieved from https://www.elpasotimes.com/story/news/local/juarez/2016/06/19/jurez-mayor-elect-vows-transparency/86064042/

Camacho, A. S. (2004). Body counts on the Mexico-U.S. border: Feminicidio, reification, and the theft of the Mexicana subjectivity. *Chicana/Latina Studies, 4*(1), 22–60.

———. (2010). Ciudadana X: Gender violence and the denationalization of women's rights in Ciudad Juárez, Mexico. In Fregoso & Bejarano (Eds.), *Terrorizing women* (pp. 275–289).

Carrera, B. (2016). The maquiladora in Ciudad Juárez: The illusion of progress. *Al Límite.* Retrieved from http://allimite.mx/2040-2/#respond

Castiglia, C., & Reed, C. (2012). *If memory serves: Gay men, AIDS, and the promise of the queer past.* Minneapolis, MN: University of Minnesota Press.

Certeau, M. de. (1988). *The practice of everyday life.* Minneapolis, MN: University of Minnesota Press.

Cevallos, D. (2004, December 03). Mexico: Two more murdered women found in Ciudad Juárez. *Interpress Service News Agency.* Retrieved from http://www.ipsnews.net/2004/12/mexico-two-more-murdered-women-found-in-ciudad-juarez/

Cheah, P. (2010). Non-dialectical materialism. In Coole & Frost (Eds.), *New materialisms* (pp. 70–91).

Chomsky, N. (1998). Notes on NAFTA: The masters of mankind. In C. Bowden (Ed.), *Juárez: The laboratory of our future* (pp. 13–20). New York, NY: Aperture.

Chow, R. (2010). The elusive material: What the dog doesn't understand. In D. Coole & S. Frost (Eds.), *New materialisms: Ontology, agency, and politics* (pp. 221–233). Durham, NC: Duke University Press.

Clare, S. (2016). On the politics of "new material feminism." In Pitts-Taylor (Ed.), *Mattering: Feminism, science and materialism* (pp. 58–72).

Cloud, D. L. (1994). The materiality of discourse as oxymoron: A challenge to critical rhetoric. *Western Journal of Communication, 58*(3), 141–163.

———. (1998). *Control and consolation in American culture and politics: Rhetorics of therapy.* Thousand Oaks, CA: Sage.

———. (2006). *The Matrix* and critical theory's desertion of the real. *Communication and Critical/Cultural Studies, 3*(4), 329–354.

———. (2009). The materialist dialectic as a site of Kairos: Theorizing rhetorical intervention in material social relations. In B. A. Biesecker & J. L. Lucaites (Eds.), *Rhetoric, materiality, & politics* (pp. 293–320). New York, NY: Peter Lang.

Cloud, D. L., & Gunn, J. (2011). Introduction: W(h)ither ideology? *Western Journal of Communication, 75*(4), 407–420.

Cloud, D. L., Macek, S., & Aune, J. A. (2006). "The limbo of ethical simulacra": A reply to Ron Greene. *Philosophy and Rhetoric, 39*(1), 72–84.

Cobo, L. (2004). Los Tigres del Norte: Music with a conscience. *Hispanic Magazine,* July/August. Retrieved from: http://www.latinamericanstudies.org/latinos/tigres. htm

Colebrook, C. (2008). On not becoming man: The materialist politics of unactualized potential. In Alaimo & Hekman (Eds.), *Material feminisms* (pp. 52–84).

Commercial-El Paso & Juarez Tourism Board. (2016). Available from Vimeo. Retrieved from https://vimeo.com/194459757

Connolly, W. E. (2010). Materialities of experience. In D. Coole & S. Frost (Eds.), *New materialisms: Ontology, agency, and politics* (pp. 178–200). Durham, NC: Duke University Press.

Continuación de investigaciones abiertas de femicidios [Continued open investigations of femicides]. (2016). *Televisa Juárez,* September 15. Retrieved from http:// www.televisajuarez.tv/noticias/20863-continua-abierta-investigacion-por-feminicidios

Coogan, D. J., & Ackerman, J. M. (2010). Introduction: The space to work in public life. In J. M. Ackerman & D. J. Coogan (Eds.), *The public work of rhetoric: Citizen-scholars and civic engagement* (pp. 1–18). Columbia, SC: University of South Carolina Press.

Coole, D. (2010). The inertia of matter and the generativity of flesh. In Coole & Frost (Eds.), *New materialisms* (pp. 92–115).

Coole, D., & Frost, S. (Eds.). (2010). *New materialisms: Ontology, agency, and politics.* Durham, NC: Duke University Press.

Corchado, A. (2007, August 23). Mexico's drug war moves north. On Point. Retrieved from: http://www.wbur.org/onpoint/2007/08/23/mexicos-drug-war-moves-north

Corcoran, P. (2016). Spike in Juárez violence driven by election, criminal vacuum. *Insight Crime,* November 22. Retrieved from http://www.insightcrime.org/ news-analysis/spike-in-violence-in-juarez-driven-by-election-vacuum

Córdoba, M. S. T. (2010). Ghost dance in Ciudad Juárez at the end/beginning of the millennium. In Gaspar de Alba & Guzmán (Eds.), *Making a KILLING* (pp. 95–120).

Corona, I. (2010). Over their dead bodies: Reading the newspapers on gender violence. In Domínguez-Ruvalcaba & Corona (Eds.), *Gender violence at the U.S.-Mexico border* (pp. 104–1127).

Corona, I., & Domínguez-Ruvalcaba, H. (2010). Gender violence: An introduction. In Domínguez-Ruvalcaba & Corona (Eds.), *Gender violence at the U.S.-Mexico border* (pp. 1–13).

Corral para crear un procesamiento especializado para las personas desaparecidas [Corral to create specialized prosecution for missing persons]. (2016). *Tiempo,*

August 30. Retrieved from http://tiempo.com.mx/noticia/50794-creara_corral_fiscalia_especia/1

Country by country: The map showing the tragic figures of feminicidios in Latin America. (2016). *BBC Mundo,* November 21. Retrieved from http://www.bbc.com/mundo/noticias-america-latina [world notices latin-america]-37828573?ocid=wsmundo.chat-apps.in-app-msg.whatsapp.trial.link1_.auin

Cvetkovich, A. (2012). *Depression: A public feeling.* Durham, NC: Duke University Press.

Denvir, D. (2015). Juárez to tourists: It's safe to come back now. *The Atlantic,* July 1. Retrieved from http://www.citylab.com/crime/2015/07/juarez-to-tourists-its-safe-to-come-back-now/397232/de Onís, K. M. (2016). "Pa' que tú lo sepas": Experiences with co-presence in Puerto Rico. In McKinnon, Asen, Chávez, & Howard (Eds.), *Text + field* (pp. 101–16).

Díaz, G. L. (2016). They repudiated reforms to the "General Law of Victims"; Require observation. *Proceso,* October 26. Retrieved from http://www.proceso.com.mx/460250/repudian-reformas-a-la-ley-general-victimas-exigen-atender-observaciones [repudiated reforms to the general law of victims, requiring attention and observation].

Dickinson, G., Ott, B. L., & Aoki, E. (2006). Spaces of remembering and forgetting: The reverent eye/I at the Plains Indian Museum. *Communication and Critical/ Cultural Studies, 3*(1), 27–47.

Domínguez-Ruvalcaba, H., & Corona, I. (Eds.). (2010). *Gender violence at the U.S.-Mexico border: Media representation and public response.* Tucson, AZ: University of Arizona Press.

Driver, A. (2015). *More or less dead: Feminicidio, haunting, and the ethics of representation in Mexico.* Tucson, AZ: University of Arizona Press.

Duarte, S. P. (2008). *If I die in Juárez.* Tucson, AZ: University of Arizona Press.

Edley, P. P., & Lozano-Reich, N. M. (2011). Democracy and the academy: Ethnographic articulations and interventions for social change. In S. Kahn & J. Lee (Eds.), *Activism and rhetoric: Theories and contexts for political engagement* (pp. 125–136). New York, NY: Routledge.

Edwards, J. (2010). The materialism of historical materialism. In Coole & Frost (Eds.), *New materialisms* (pp. 281–298).

Ellingwood, K. (2009). In a Mexico state, openness is the new order in the courts. *Los Angeles Times,* February 6. Retrieved from http://www.latimes.com/world/la-fg-mexico-drugs-courtreform6-2009feb06-story.html

Endres, D., & Senda-Cook, S. (2011). Location matters: The rhetoric of place and protest. *Quarterly Journal of Speech, 97*(3), 257–282.

Ensalaco, M. (2006). Murder in Ciudad Juárez: A parable of women's struggle for human rights. *Violence Against Women, 12*(5), 417–440.

Fleckenstein, K. S. (2016). Materiality's rhetorical work: The nineteenth-century parlor stereoscope and the second-naturing of vision. In S. Barnett & C. Boyle (Eds.),

Rhetoric through everyday things (pp. 125–138). Tuscaloosa, AL: University of Alabama Press.

Forgacs, D. (2000). *The Gramsci reader: Selected writings, 1916–1935*. New York: New York University Press.

Foss, K. A., & Domenici, K. L. (2001). Haunting Argentina: Synecdoche in the protests of the Mothers of the Plaza de Mayo. *Quarterly Journal of Speech, 87*(3), 237–258.

Foucault, M. (1980). *Power/knowledge: Selected interviews and other writings, 1972–1977*. New York: Pantheon Books.

Fragoso, J. M. (2003). Serial sexual feminicidio in Ciudad Juárez, 1993–2001. *Aztlán, 28*(2), 153–178.

Fragoso, J. E. M. (2010). The victims of Ciudad Juárez feminicidio: Sexually fetishized commodities. In Fregoso & Bejarano (Eds.), *Terrorizing women* (pp. 59–69).

Fregoso, R. L. (2000). Voices without echo: The global gendered apartheid. *Emergences, 10*(1), 137–155.

———. (2000). Voices without echo: The global gendered apartheid. *Emergences, 10*(1), 137–155.

———. (2006). "We want them alive!" The politics and culture of human rights. *Social Identities, 12*(2), 109–138.

Fregoso, R.-L., & Bejarano, C. (Eds.) (2010). *Terrorizing women: Feminicidio in the Américas*. Durham, NC: Duke University Press.

Frontera NorteSur. (2016, April). Ciudad Juarez commercial/entertainment district bounces back. Retrieved from https://fnsnews.nmsu.edu/ciudad-juarez-commercialentertainment-district-bounces-back/

Frost, S. (2010). Fear and the illusion of autonomy. In D. Coole & S. Frost (Eds.), *New materialisms: Ontology, agency, and the politics* (pp. 158–77). Durham, NC: Duke University Press.

Gabor, M. (2016, October). Feminicidio: Not one more. *Council on Hemispheric Affairs*. Retrieved from http://www.coha.org/feminicidio-not-one-more/

Gabrielson, T. (2016). The enactment of intention and exception through poisoned corpses and toxic bodies. In V. Pitts-Taylor (Ed.), *Mattering: Feminism, science, and materialism* (pp. 173–87). New York: New York University Press.

Garcia-del Moral, P. (2015). Transforming feminicidio: Framing, institutionalization and social change. *Current Sociology*, 1–19.

Gaspar de Alba, A. (2005). *Desert blood: The Juárez murders*. Houston, TX: Arte Público.

———. (2010). Poor brown female: The Miller's compensation for "free" trade. In A. Gaspar de Alba & G. Guzmán (Eds.), *Making a KILLING: Femicide, Free Trade, and la frontera* (pp. 63–94). Austin, TX: University of Texas Press.

Gaspar de Alba, A. & Guzmán, G. (Eds.). (2010b). *Making a KILLING: Feminicidio, free trade, and la frontera*. Austin, TX: University of Texas Press.

Gender alert declared in 41 municipalities. (2016). *Mexico News Daily*, July 2. Retrieved from http://mexiconewsdaily.com/news/violence-against-women/

Gibler, J. (2011). *To die in Mexico: Dispatches from inside the drug war.* San Francisco, CA: City Lights Books.

Goñi, U. (2016). Argentina's women joined across South America in marches against violence. *The Guardian*, October 20. Retrieved from https://www.theguardian.com/world/2016/oct/20/argentina-women-south-america-marches-violence-ni-una-menos

González et al. ("Cotton Field") v. Mexico. (2009). Inter-American Court of Human Rights (IACrtHR), 16 November 2009.

Gordon, A. F. (1997). *Ghostly matters: Haunting and the sociological imagination.* Minneapolis, MN: University of Minnesota Press.

———. (2008). *Ghostly matters: Haunting and the sociological imagination.* Minneapolis, MN: University of Minnesota Press.

Gramsci, A. (1971). Selections from the prison notebooks. In B. B. Lawrence & A. Karim (Eds.), *On violence: A reader* (pp. 158–179). Durham, NC: Duke University Press.

Greene, R. W. (1998). Another materialist rhetoric. *Critical Studies in Mass Communication, 15,* 21–41.

———. (2004). Rhetoric and capitalism: Rhetorical agency as communicative labor. *Philosophy and Rhetoric, 37*(3), 188–206.

———. (2006). Orator Communist. *Philosophy and Rhetoric, 39*(1), 85–95.

———. (2010). Spatial materialism: Labor, location, and transnational literacy. *Critical Studies in Media Communication, 27*(1), 105–110.

———. (2015). More materialist rhetoric. *Communication and Critical/Cultural Studies, 12*(4), 1–4.

Gries, L. (2016). On rhetorical becoming. In S. Barnett & C. Boyle (Eds.), *Rhetoric through everyday things* (pp. 155–170). Tuscaloosa, AL: University of Alabama Press.

Gronbeck, R. (2009). Jacob Riis and the doubly material rhetorics of his politics. In B. A. Biesecker & J. L. Lucaites (Eds.), *Rhetoric, materiality, & Politics* (pp. 131–160). New York: Peter Lang Publishing, Inc.

Grosz, E. (1994). *Volatile bodies: Toward a corporeal feminism.* Bloomington, IN: Indiana University Press.

———. (2010). Feminism, materialism, and freedom. In Coole & Frost (Eds.), *New materialisms* (pp. 139–157).

Haraway, D. J. (2008). Otherwordly conversations, terrain topics, local terms. In Alaimo & Hekman (Eds.), *Material feminisms* (pp. 157–187).

Harding, S. (1991). *Whose science? Whose knowledge? Thinking from women's lives.* Ithaca, NY: Cornell University Press.

Harrington, J. C. (2015). ¡Alto a la Impunidad! Is there legal relief for the murders of women in Ciudad Juárez? In Domínguez-Ruvalcaba & Corona (Eds.), *Gender violence at the U.S.–Mexico border* (pp. 154–176).

Harris, K. L. (2015). Feminist dilemmatic theorizing: New materialism in communication studies. *Communication Theory*, 1–21.

Haskins, E. (2011). *Global memoryscapes: Contesting remembrance in a transnational age.* Tuscaloosa, AL: University of Alabama Press.

Hawken, S. (2011). *The dead women of Juárez.* London: Serpent's Tail.

———. (2013). *The Juárez dance.* San Bernardino, CA: Pax River Books.

Hennessey, R. (1993). *Materialist feminism and the politics of discourse.* New York, NY: Routledge.

Hernandez, S. (2004). Family cries out for punishment of the murderer. *El Norte,* November 5, p. 8A.

Hesford, W. (2011). *Spectacular rhetorics: Human rights visions, recognitions, feminisms.* Durham, NC: Duke University Press.

Hesford, W. S., & Kozol, W. (Eds.). (2005). *Just advocacy? Women's human rights, transnational feminism, and the politics of representation.* New Brunswick, NJ: Rutgers University Press.

Hess, A. (2016). Embodied judgment: A call for a phronetic orientation in rhetorical ethnography. In McKinnon, Asen, Chávez, & Howard (Eds.), *Text + field* (pp. 86–100).

Hill Collins, P. (1986). Learning from the outsider within: The sociological significance of Black feminist thought. *Social Problems, 33*(6), S14–S32.

Hing, B. O. (2010). *Ethical borders: NAFTA, globalization and Mexican migration.* Philadelphia: Temple University Press.

Hise, S. (Prod.), & Hise, S. (Dir.). (2006). *On the edge: The feminicidio in Ciudad Juárez* [Documentary]. United States: Detrital Films.

Holling, M. A. (2014). "So my name is Alma and I am the sister of . . .": A feminicidio testimonio of violence and violent identifications. *Women's Studies in Communication, 37,* 313–338.

Human Rights Watch. (2007). *World report: Events of 2006.* New York, NY: Author.

Iturralde, C. (2010). Searching for accountability on the border: Justice for the women of Ciudad Juárez. In Fregoso & Bejarano (Eds.), *Terrorizing women* (pp. 243–262).

Kruks, S. (2010). Simone de Beauvoir: Engaging discrepant materialism. In Coole & Frost (Eds.), *New materialisms* (pp. 258–280).

Laclau, E., & Mouffe, C. (1985). *Hegemony and socialist strategy: Towards a radical democratic politics.* London, UK: Verso (New Left).

Lagarde y de los Ríos, M. M. (2010). Preface: Feminist keys for understanding feminicide theoretical, political, and legal construction. In R. L. Fregosa & C. Bejarano (Eds.), *Terrorizing women: Feminicide in the Américas* (pp. xi–xxvi). Durham, NC: Duke University Press.

La Haye, Y. de (1979). Introduction. In Yves de la Haye (Ed.), *Marx & Engels on the means of communication: The movement of commodities, people, information & capital* (pp. 9–56). Bagnolet, France: International General and Yves de la Haye.

Landau, J. (2016). Feeling rhetorical critics: Another affective-emotional field method for rhetorical studies. In McKinnon, Asen, Chávez, & Howard (Eds.), *Text + field* (pp. 72–85).

LaRose, A. (2015). *Juárez: Seeds in the desert*. Author.

Las Mujeres LLC (Prod.), & Dobson, K. J. (Dir.). (2006). *The virgin of Juárez* [Motion picture]. Spain: Eurocine Films.

Latour, B. (1999). *Pandora's Box: Essays on the reality of science studies*. Cambridge, MA: Harvard University Press.

Lefebvre, H. (1991). *The production of space* (D. Nicholson-Smith, Trans.). Oxford: Blackwell.

———. (2002). *Critique of everyday life* (J. Moore, Trans.). New York, NY: Verso.

Levinas, E. (1985). *Ethics and infinity: Conversations with Philippe Nemo* (R. A. Cohen, Trans.). Pittsburgh, PA: Duquesne University Press.

———. (1985). *Ethics and infinity*. Pittsburgh, PA: Duquesne University Press.

Lindsay, D. (2008). *Lost in Juárez*. Inverness, Scotland: Long Midnight.

Livingston, J. (2004). Murder in Juárez: Gender, sexual violence, and the global assembly line. *Frontiers, 25*(1), 59–76.

López, A. C., Caballero, A. G., & Rodríguez, L. C. (2010). Feminicidio in Latin America and the movement for women's human rights. In Fregoso & Bejarano (Eds.), *Terrorizing women* (pp. 157–178).

López, J. I. A. (2012). The Cotton Field case: Gender perspective and feminist theories in the Inter-American Court of Human Rights jurisprudence. *International Law, 21*, 17–54.

López-Lozano, M. (2010). Women in the global machine: Patrick Bard's *La frontera*, Carmen Galán Benítez's *Tierra marchita*, and Alicia Gaspar de Alba's *Desert Blood: The Juárez Murders*. In Domínguez-Ruvalcaba & Corona (Eds.), *Gender violence at the U.S.–Mexico border* (pp. 128–153).

Los Tigres del Norte. (2004). Las mujeres de Juárez. *Pacto de Sangre* [CD]. MX: Fonovisa.

Luévano, R. (2012). *Woman-killing in Juárez: Theodicy at the border*. Maryknoll, NY: Orbis Books.

Luján, F. (2016). Cabada: Incrementar el presupuesto para el Instituto de la Mujer [Cabada: Increase the budget for the Institute of Women]. *Norte Digital*, November 25. Retrieved from http://nortedigital.mx/cabada-aumentara-presupuesto-instituto-la-mujer/

MacKinnon, C. A. (1994). Rape, genocide, and women's human rights. *Harvard Women's Law Journal, 17*, 5–16.

Malloy, M. (2014, January 09). Q & A with Molly Malloy: The story of the Juárez fem-icides is a myth. *Texas Observer.* Retrieved from: https://www.texasobserver.org/qa-molly-molloy-story-juarez-femicides-myth/

Maquiladora workers in Juárez form a union. (2016). *Living Wage,* February. Retrieved from http://www.livingwage-sf.org/fair-trade/maquiladora-workers-in-juarez-form-a-union/

Marx, K. (1844). *Economic and philosophic manuscripts of 1844.* New York: Pro-metheus Books.

———. (1844/1977). *Capital: A critique of political economy* (Vol. 2). New York, NY: Vintage.

———. (1978). *The Marx-Engels Reader.* New York: Norton.

Marx, K., & Engels, F. (2005). *The communist manifesto.* New York: International.

May, M. S. (2015). The imaginative-power of "another materialist rhetoric." *Communication and Critical/Cultural Studies, 12*(4), 399–403.

Mbembe, A. (2003). Necropolitics. *Public Culture, 15*(1), 11–40.

McCann, B. J. (2016). "Chrysler pulled the trigger": The affective politics of insanity and Black rage at the trial of James Johnson, Jr. *Rhetoric Society Quarterly, 46*(2), 131–155.

McDonnell, P. J. (2016). "Mexico is one big cemetery": The search for the secret graves of "the disappeared." *Los Angeles Times,* September 29. Retrieved from http://www.latimes.com/world/mexico-americas/la-fg-mexico-missing-20160929-snap-story.html

McGee, M. C. (1982). A materialist's conception of rhetoric. In R. E. McKerrow (Ed.), *Explorations in rhetoric* (pp. 23–48). Glenview, IL: Scott, Foresman.

McKinnon, S. (2010). (In)hospitable publics: Theorizing modalities of access to U.S. publics. In D. C. Brouwer & R. Asen (Eds.), *Public modalities: Rhetoric, culture, media, and the shape of public life* (pp. 131–153). Tuscaloosa, AL: University of Alabama Press.

McKinnon, S. L., Asen, R., Chávez, K. R., & Howard, R. G. (Eds.). (2016). *Text + field: Innovations in rhetorical method.* University Park, PA: Pennsylvania State University Press.

McNely, B. J. (2016). Circulatory intensities: Take a book, return a book. In S. Barnett & C. Boyle (Eds.), *Rhetoric through everyday things* (pp. 139–154). Tuscaloosa, AL: University of Alabama Press.

Meibner, H. (2016). New material feminism and historical materialism: A diffractive reading of two (ostensibly) unrelated perspectives. In Pitts-Taylor (Ed.), *Mattering: Feminism, science and materialism* (pp. 43–57).

Mexican state issues "gender alert" to address feminicide. (2016). *Telesur,* February 8. Retrieved from http://www.telesurtv.net/english/news/Mexican-State-Issues-Gender-Alert-to-Address-Feminicidio-20160208-0005.html

Mexico Solidarity Network. (2003). *Feminicidios of Ciudad Juárez & Chihuahua.* Red de Solidaridad con Mexico. Chicago, IL: Author.

Mexico's monthly murder rate reaches 20-year high. (2017). *The Guardian,* June 21. Retrieved from https://www.theguardian.com/world/2017/jun/21/mexicos-monthly-rate-reaches-20-year-high

Mohanty, C. T. (1997). Women workers and capitalist scripts: Ideologies of domination, common interests, and the politics of solidarity. In M. J. Alexander & C. T. Mohanty (Eds), *Feminist genealogies, colonial legacies, democratic futures* (pp. 3–29). New York, NY: Routledge.

Monárrez-Fragoso, J. E. (1998–present). *Feminicidio Data Base* [particular investigation file], Ciudad Juárez, Cultural Studies Department, Dirección General Noroeste, el Colegio de la Frontera Norte.

———. (2010). The suffering of the other. In Gaspar de Alba & Guzmán (Eds.), *Making a KILLING* (pp. 183–200).

Morfín, G. (2004). *Informe de gestión: Noviembre 2003–Abril 2004.* Cd. Juárez: Comisión para Prevenir y Eradicar la Violencia Contra las Mujeres in Ciudad Juárez. Secretaría de Gebernanción (SEGOB).

Morris, C. E. III. (2004). My old Kentucky homo: Lincoln and the politics of queer public memory. In. K. R. Phillips (Ed.), *Framing public memory.* Tuscaloosa, AL: The University of Alabama Press.

Mueller, C., Hansen, M., & Qualtire, K. (2009). Feminicidio on the border and new forms of protest. In K. Staudt, T. Payan, & A. Kruszewski,(Eds.), *Human rights along the U.S.–Mexico border: Gendered violence and insecurity* (pp. 125–149). Tucson, AZ: University of Arizona Press.

Negt, O. (1988). What is a revival of Marxism and why do we need one today? Centennial lecture commemorating the death of Karl Marx. In C. Nelson & L. Grossberg (Eds.), *Marxism and the interpretation of* culture (pp. 211–234). Chicago, IL: University of Illinois Press.

Nieto, Y. (2016). 42 bones are found in the Arroyo del Navajo. *Entrelíneas,* September 20. Retrieved from http://entrelineas.com.mx/local/encuentran-42-restos-oseos-en-el-arroyo-de-el-navajo/ [42 bones are found in the Arroyo del Navajo].

Nieves, A. D. (2002). "With them the pen must be mightier than the sword": Writing, engendering, and racializing planning history. *Journal of Planning History, 1*(3), 215–219.

Olivera, M. (2010). Violencia Feminicida: Violence against women and Mexico's structural crisis. In Fregoso & Bejarano (Eds.), *Terrorizing women* (pp. 49–58).

Orlie, M. A. (2010). Impersonal matter. In D. Coole & S. Frost (Eds.), *New materialisms: Ontology, agency, and politics* (pp. 116–38). Durham, NC: Duke University Press.

Ortiz, M. (2016, July 7). Ciclos de Violencia. [Cycles of violence] [Facebook post]. Retrieved from https://www.facebook.com/MARISELAORTIZnhdrc/posts/1400266943333562

Pflugfelder, E. H. (2015). Rhetoric's new materialism: From micro-rhetoric to micro-brew. *Rhetoric Society Quarterly, 45*(5), 441–461.

Phelan, P. (1993). *Unmarked: The politics of performance.* New York, NY: Routledge.

Phillips, K. R. (Ed.). (2004). *Framing public memory.* Tuscaloosa, AL: University of Alabama Press.

———. (2010). The failure of memory: Reflections on rhetoric and public remembrance. *Western Journal of Communication, 74*(2), 208–223.

Phillips, K. R., & Reyes, G. M. (2011). *Global memoryscapes: Contesting remembrance in a transnational age.* Tuscaloosa, AL: University of Alabama Press.

Pineda-Madrid, N. (2011). *Suffering and salvation in Ciudad Juárez.* Minneapolis, MN: Fortress.

Pink, S. (2012). *Situating everyday life: Practices and places.* Los Angeles, CA: Sage.

Pitts-Taylor, V. (Ed). (2016). *Mattering: Feminism, science and materialism.* New York, NY: New York University Press.

Portillo, L. (Dir.). (2001). *Señorita extraviada.* [Documentary] Independent Television Service. Xochitl Films.

Prado, H. M. (2016). Corral se compromete con las familias de las víctimas. [Corral commits to families of victims]. *Norte Digital,* November 26. Retrieved from http://nortedigital.mx/se-compromete-corral-familias-victimas/

Prieto, N. I. (1999). *Beautiful flowers of the maquiladora: Life histories of women workers in Tijuana.* Austin, TX: University of Texas Press.

Pruchnic, J. & Lacey, K. (2011). The future of forgetting: Rhetoric, memory, affect. *Rhetoric Society Quarterly, 41*(5), 472–494.

Quinones, S. (2016). Once the world's most dangerous city, Juárez returns to life. *National Geographic,* June. Retrieved from http://www.nationalgeographic.com/magazine/2016/06/juarez-mexico-border-city-drug-cartels-murder-revival/

Radford, J. (1992). Introduction. In J. Radford & D. E H. Russell (Eds.), *Femicide: The politics of woman killing* (pp. 3–12). New York, NY: Twayne.

Radford, J., & Russell, D. E. H. (Eds.). (1992). *Femicide: The politics of woman killing.* New York, NY: Twayne.

Rand, E. J. (2015). Bad feelings in public: Rhetoric, affect, and emotion. *Rhetoric & Public Affairs, 18*(1), 161–175.

Rickert, T. (2013). *Ambient rhetoric: The attunements of rhetorical being.* Pittsburgh, PA: University of Pittsburgh Press.

Rodriguez, T. *The daughters of Juárez.* New York: Atria Books.

Rodriguez, T., Montané, D., & Pulitzer, L. (2007). *The daughters of Juárez: A true story of serial murder south of the border.* New York, NY: Atria Books.

Roig-Franzia, M. (2007). In Juárez: Expiring justice. *Washington Post,* May 14. Retrieved from http://www.washingtonpost.com/wp-dyn/content/article/2007/05/13/AR2007051301334.html

Rojas, C. E. (2010). The V-Day march in Mexico: Appropriation and misuse of local women's activism. In Gaspar de Alba & Guzmán (Eds.), *Making a KILLING* (pp. 201–210).

Román, J. A. (2016). La ONU exige en México que los militares abandonen las tareas de seguridad pública. [UN demands in Mexico that military leave public security tasks]. *La Jornada*, November 24. Retrieved from http://www.jornada.unam.mx/ultimas/2016/11/24/pide-onu-en-mexico-que-militares-abandonen-tareas-de-seguridad

Roy, D., & Subramaniam, B. (2016). Matter in the shadows: Feminist new materialism and the practices of colonialism. In Pitts-Taylor (Ed.), *Mattering: Feminism, science and materialism* (pp. 23–42).

Russell, D. E. H. (2001). Defining femicide and related concepts. In D. E. H. Russell & R. A. Harmes (Eds.), *Femicide in global perspective* (pp. 12–28). New York, NY: Teachers College Press.

———. (2001). Introduction: The politics of femicide. In D. E. H. Russell & R. A. Harmes (Eds.), *Femicide in global perspective* (pp. 3–11). New York, NY: Teachers College Press.

Salzinger, L. (2003). *Genders in production*. Berkeley, CA: University of California Press.

Schiappa, E. (2015). What hath Greene wrought? *Communication and Critical/Cultural Studies, 12*(4), 397–398.

Schmidt Camacho, A. (2004). Body counts on the Mexico–U.S. border: Feminicidio, reification, and the theft of Mexicana subjectivity. *Chicana/Latina Studies, 4*(1), 22–60.

Segato, R. L. (2010). Territory, sovereignty, and crimes of the second state: The writing on the body of murdered women. In Fregoso & Bejarano (Eds.), *Terrorizing women* (pp. 70–92).

Seigworth, G., & Gregg, M. (2010). An inventory of shimmers. In G. Seigworth & M. Gregg (Eds.), *The affect theory reader* (pp. 1–25). Durham, NC: Duke University Press.

Semuels, A. (2016). Upheaval in the factories of Juárez. *The Atlantic*, January 21. Retrieved from https://www.theatlantic.com/business/archive/2016/01/upheaval-in-the-factories-of-juarez/424893/

Senda-Cook, S., Middleton, M. K., & Endres, D. (2016). Interrogating the "field." In McKinnon, Asen, Chávez, & Howard (Eds.), *Text + field* (pp. 22–39).

Shome, R. (2003). Space matters: The power and practice of space. *International Communication Association, 13*(1), 39–56.

Simmons, P. W., & Coplan, R. (2010). Innovative transnational remedies for the women of Ciudad Juárez. In Fregoso & Bejarano (Eds.), *Terrorizing women* (pp. 197–224).

Sloop, J. M. (2015). Illuminating Greene's materialist rhetoric. *Communication and Critical Cultural Studies, 12*(4), 410–413.

Staudt, K. (2000). Globalization and gender at border sites: Feminicidio and domestic violence in Ciudad Juárez. In M. H. Marchand & A. S. Runyan (Eds.), *Gender and global restructuring: Sightings, sites and resistances* (pp. 187–222). London: Routledge.

———. (2008). *Violence and activism at the border: Gender, fear and everyday life in Ciudad Juárez.* Austin, TX: University of Texas Press.

———. (2009a). Violence against women at the border: Unpacking institutions. In Staudt, Payan, & Kruszewski (Eds.), *Human rights along the U.S.–Mexico border* (pp. 107–124).

———. (2009b). Violence at the border: Broadening the discourse to include feminism, human security, and deeper democracy. In Staudt, Payan, & Kruszewski (Eds.), *Human rights along the U.S.–Mexico border* (pp. 1–27).

Staudt, K., & Coronado, I. (2002). *Fronteras no más: Toward social justice at the U.S.–Mexico border.* New York: Palgrave Macmillan.

———. (2010). Binational civic action for accountability: Antiviolence organizing in Ciudad Juárez / El Paso. In Gaspar de Alba & Guzmán (Eds.), *Making a KILLING* (pp. 157–182).

Staudt, K., Fuentes, C., & Fragoso, J. M. (Eds.). (2010). *Cities and citizenship at the U.S.–Mexico border: The Paso del Norte metropolitan region.* New York, NY: Palgrave Macmillan.

Staudt, K., & Méndez, Z. Y. (2015). *Courage, resistance & women in Ciudad Juárez: Challenges to militarization.* Austin, TX: University of Texas Press.

Staudt, K., Payan, T., & Kruszewski, Z. A. (2009). *Human rights along the U.S.–Mexico border: Gendered violence and insecurity.* Tucson, AZ: University of Arizona Press.

Suicide in Ciudad Juarez: Where life has little value. (2017). *BBC News,* February 5. Retrieved from http://www.bbc.com/news/world-latin-america-38826400

Swenson, K. A. (2015). Being in common: In celebration of Ronald W. Greene's Woolbert Award. *Communication and Critical/Cultural Studies,* 12(4), 404–409.

Taylor, D. (1997). *Disappearing acts: Spectacles of gender and nationalism in Argentina's "dirty war."* Durham, NC: Duke University Press.

Taylor, V. (2015). Human rights and human security: Feminists contesting the terrain. In R. Baksh & W. Harcourt (Eds.), *The Oxford handbook of transnational feminist movements* (pp. 346–366). Oxford: Oxford University Press.

Tomlinson, B. (2010). *Feminism and affect at the scene of argument: Beyond the trope of the angry feminist.* Philadelphia, PA: Temple University Press.

Valdez, D. W. (2006). *The killing field harvest of women: The truth about Mexico's bloody border legacy.* Burbank, CA: Peace at the Border.

Valencia, N. (2015). After years of violence and death, "life is back" in Juárez. *CNN,* April 21. Retrieved from http://www.cnn.com/2015/04/21/americas/mexico-ciudad-juarez-tourism/

Villagran, L. (2016). Juárez murders up for 1st time since drug war. *Albuquerque Journal,* December 26. Retrieved from https://www.abqjournal.com/915667/juaacutere-zmurders-up-for-1st-time-since-drug-war.html

Vivian, B. (2004). "A timeless now": Memory and repetition. In K. R. Phillips (Ed.), *Framing public memory* (pp. 187–211). Tuscaloosa, AL: University of Alabama Press.

Volk, S. S., & Schlotterbeck, M. E. (2010). Gender, order, and feminicidio: Reading the popular culture of murder in Ciudad Juárez. In Gaspar de Alba & Guzmán (Eds.), *Making a KILLING* (pp. 121–154).

Washick, B., & Wingrove, E. (2015). Politics that matter: Thinking about power and justice with the new materialists. *Contemporary Political Theory, 14,* 63–89.

Weissman, D. M. (2010). Global economics and their progenies: Theorizing feminicidio in context. In Fregoso & Bejarano (Eds.), *Terrorizing women* (pp. 225–242).

Welsome, E. (2007, May 04). Eminent disaster. *Texas Observer.* Retrieved from: https://www.texasobserver.org/2483-eminent-disaster-a-cabal-of-politicians-and-profiteers-targets-an-el-paso-barrio/

———. (2007). Lomas Del Poleo: A three-part series. Pasodelsur. Retrieved from http://www.eileenwelsome.com/lomas-del-poleo/

Winter, J. (1995). *Sites of memory, sites of mourning: The great war in European cultural history.* Cambridge, UK: Cambridge University Press.

Wirth-Cauchon, J. (2016). Nonlinear evolution, sexual difference, and the ontological turn: Elizabeth Grosz's reading of Darwin. In. V. Pitts-Taylor (Ed.), *MATTERING: Feminism, science, and materialism.* New York: New York University Press.

Wise, R. D. (2006). Migration and imperialism: The Mexican workforce in the context of NAFTA. *Latin American Perspectives, 33*(2), 33–45.

Wright, E. A. (2005). Rhetorical spaces in memorial places: The cemetery in a rhetorical memory place/space, *Rhetoric Society Quarterly, 35*(4), 51–81.

Wright, M. W. (1999). The dialectics of still life: Murder, women and the maquiladoras. *Public Culture, 11*(3), 453–74.

———. (2001a). Feminine villains, masculine heroes, and the reproduction of Ciudad Juárez. *Social Text, 19*(4), 93–113.

———. (2001b). A manifesto against femicide. *Antipode, 33,* 550–566.

———. (2004). From protests to politics: Sex work, women's worth, and Ciudad Juárez modernity. *Annals of the Association of American Geographers, 94*(2), 369–386.

———. (2006). *Disposable women and other myths of global capitalism.* New York, NY: Routledge.

———. (2010a). Mother-activism, and the geography of protest in northern Mexico. In Gaspar de Alba & Guzmán (Eds.), *Making a KILLING* (pp. 211–242).

———. (2010b). Paradoxes, protests, and the Mujeres de Negro of Northern Mexico. In Fregoso & Bejarano (Eds.), *Terrorizing women* (pp. 312–330).

———. (2011). Necropolitics, narcopolitics, and femicide: Gendered violence on the Mexico-U.S. border. *Signs, 36*(3), 707–731.

Zelizer, B. (2002). Finding aids to the past: Bearing personal witness to traumatic public events. *Media, Culture & Society, 24,* 697–714.

INDEX

Acequia Madre, 79, 80 fig. 3.3

ADC Factory, 132

agency, 4–9, 46, 66–69, 85–86, 107–8, 134–36

Aguirre González, Perla Ivonne, 108n1

Alanis, Monica, 93 fig. 4.2, 93–94

Alanis Esparza, Monica Janeth, 108n1

Alba Protocol, 125, 125n1

Alta Vista Preparatory School, 98, 106

Amavizca, Rubén, xvii

American Convention on Human Rights, 34

Amos, Tori, xvii

Anapra, 61, 64, 64n10

Andrade García, Norma Estela, 21, 26

Arce, Evangelina, 25, 29, plate 13

Arce, Silvia, 25

Argentina, 74–75, 89

Argentinian Forensic Anthropology Team (EAAF), 34–35

Arroyo del Navajo, 108–21, 108n1, 113 fig. 5.1, 115n3, 117 fig. 5.2, 131, plate 8–plate 9, plate 11–plate 12

assassination, xxiii, 30, 40–41, 41 fig. 1.2, 55–56, 89

assemblages, 46–48, 52, 65–68

Autonomous University of Social Movements (AUSM), 63n8

Azucena, Neyra, 14–15, 24, 29, 30 fig. 1.1, 31–32, 78

Blanco, J., 128

Border Industrial Program, 49

border materialism, 1–2, 135–36; activism and, 123, 133; defined, 8; as new direction, 8–9

Bordertown (film), xvii

Bosnia-Herzegovina, xxiii

Bracero program, 48–50

Bring Our Daughters Home, 55–56

bureaucracy, 25. See also government

bus stops, 27, 83

Butler, Judith, 104–5, 113

Cabada, Armando, 129
Camino Real, 48–49, 76
Campo Algodonero, 33–34, 54–55, 55n4
capitalism, 8, 91, 109–10, 134. *See also* neoliberalism
Caraveo, Victoria, 27, 58–59, 125
Cardenas, Macrina, 52, 57
Carrera, Benjamin, 63, 63n9, 133
Carrillo, Enriquez, Nohemi, 28
Castañeda, Cinthia Jocabeth, 36, 43, 94–95, 95 fig. 4.3
Castañeda, Karla, 36, 43, 94–95, 95 fig. 4.3, 114
Castillo, Brenda Berenice, 108n1
Castillo, José Luis, 44, 78–79, 80 fig. 3.3, 82–83, 84 fig. 3.4, 87, 98, 111, 116–19, 119n6, 128–31, plate 12
Castillo Rincón, Esmeralda, 44, 44n12, 83, 84 fig. 3.4, 87, 90–91, 92 fig. 4.1, 108n1, 111
Castro, Lucha, 33–34
Celis Murrillo, Jazmin Tailen, 108n1
Center for Women's Rights, 126
Cervantes, Patricia, 24, 29, 31–32, 78
Chavez Caldera, Maria Elena, 10, 35, 95–96, 98, 104, 106
Chavez Cano, Esther, xviii, 22n1
Chávez Villanueva, Paola, 124
chupacabra, xvii
citizen action committees, 110–11. *See also* "Mother-activist" groups
class: intersectionality of gender and, 40, 42
Colegio de la Frontera Norte (COLEF), 36
colónias, 41 fig. 1.2, 47, 52, 53 fig. 2.1, 61, 63–65, 82n3
"Commission for the Prevention and Eradication of Violence Against Women in Ciudad Juárez," 35–36
Commscope, 53n3, 132

confession: via torture, 31–32
Contreras, Julián, 38–42, 45, 48n1, 130
co-presence, 12–13
Corchado, Verónica, 130
Cordero, Lydia, 58, 58n6
Corral Jurado, Javier, 124–27
corruption, fig. 1.1, 29–31, 38, 50, 123, 130. *See also* government
Cosyddhac, 126
"cotton field" case (Inter-American Court of Human Rights), 33–34, 124–25
"cotton field" monument, 71–74, 73 fig. 3.1
crime, organized, 40, 42, 110, 125–26
crosses, 70–72, 75–80, 76 fig. 3.2, 80 fig. 3.3, 87–88, plate 2–plate 3, plate 9
Cuba, 63n8
Cuernos de la Luna, 14–15
cultural gendered norms, 127–29

"dark legend," xvii, 43–44
de Certeau, Michel, 97
disposable, 50–51, 56–57
DNA, 24, 34–35, 114–15, 117, 121–22
"doll therapy," 27
Dominguez, Virginia Elizabeth, 108n1
"double life" charges, about victims by government, 27–29
Driver, Minnie, xvii

El Barzón de Chihuahua, 22
Engels, Friedrich, 52
Enriquez, Hortensia, 28
Ensler, Eve, xvii
Escobedo, Ruby, 37
Escobedo Ortiz, Marisela, 22–23, 32–33, 37–38, 55–56, 58, 89–90
Esquina Ortiz, Lilia Berenice, 108n1
Estrella, Airis, 101, 101n4
eyes, 93–94

face, 91

"Faces of Feminicidio" murals, 87, 92 fig. 4.1, 93 fig. 4.2, 95 fig. 4.3, 97 fig. 4.4, 105–6; as "guardians of the barrio," 101, 101n4; as haunting, 88–98; locations of, 88; and object-oriented affect, 89, 100–103; origins of, 87–88; promulgating effect of, 98–100; as protectors, 89, 98–100

falsification of evidence, 24

femicide: defined, xxii–xxiii. See also *feminicidio*

Femicide: The Politics of Woman Killing (Radford and Russell), xxii

feminicidio: as legal category, 124–27; as myth, xvii, 43; as term, xxiii; Wave One, 19–20; Wave Two, 21–36; Wave Three, 37–43; Wave Four, 43–45

Ferrel Rivera, Flor Fabiola, 99, 102, 102n5

Field, Sally, xvii

Flores, Paula, 20, 75, 80 fig. 3.3, 91, 102–3

Fonda, Jane, xvii

forensics team, Argentinian, 34–35

fountains, 82, 82n3, plate 10

Fraire Jaquez, Yanira, 108n1

Frayre, Ruby, 37, 89–90

Frenté Marginal, 44–45, 48n1, 81, 111, 129

Galarza Judith, 20, 126, 126n2

Garcia, Lizbeth Aviles, 108n1

Garcia, Rosa, 112–13

García Andrade, Lilia Alejandra, 21

Gardena Villalobos, Ana Maria, 101, 101n4

gender: and *feminicidio* as term, xxiii; intersectionality of, and class, 42; roles, 128–29; sensitivity, 34, 36

gender alerts, xxii, 125

gendered norms: cultural, 127–29; disruption of, 57–59

Gómez, Alma, 22–23, 22n1, 76–77

González, Claudia Ivette, 33–34, 55n5

González, Irma, 74, 127

González, Josefina, 55, 55n5

González, Julieta Marlen, 27

González, Santiago, 108n1

González et al. "Cotton Field" vs. Mexico, 33–34

González Flores, Sagrario, 75, 96–97, 97 fig. 4.4, 106

González Vargas, Marisela, 102–3

government: and activist purges, 40–41; antagonism with "Mother-activist" groups, 21, 23–24; bureaucracy, 25; corruption, fig. 1.1, 29–31; denials by, 43–44; division tactics of, with "Mother-activist" groups, 26; "double life" charges by, about victims, 27–29; enactment of role of, and vibrant matter, 112–14; falsification of evidence by, 24, 114–15; frustration with, 112–13; harassment by, 13, 24–25, 34, 64, 75, 116n3, 121, plate 4; hysteria charges by, of "Mother-activist" groups, 26–27; intimidation by, 75, 120–21, plate 4; involvement in crimes, fig. 1.1, 29–31; and militarization, 37–39; monuments, 70–74, 73 fig. 3.1; necropolitics and, 37–38; organized crime and, 125–26; pressure on, 129–31; refusal to search by, 27–29; scapegoating by, 31–32; torture by, for confession, 31–32

government murals, 103–5, 105n6

Gramsci, Antonio, 23

Grupo de Acción por los Derechos Hermanos y la Justicia Social, 44

Grupo Vida, 111, 114–15

Guerrero, xxii

Guerrero, Luis, 64n10

Guerrero Venzor, Andrea, 108n1

Hansen, Tom, 63, 63n8

harassment, government, 13, 24–25, 34, 64, 75, 116n3, 121, plate 4

haunting, 88–98, 131–32

Hernández, Marisela Avila, 108n1

Hernández Cano, Rose Virginia, 90–91, 92 fig. 4.1

Hernández Trejo, Beatriz Alejandra, 108n1

Herrera Montreal, Esmeralda, 33–34

highway, 64, 64n10

Hormigas, Las, 65, 66n11, 133, plate 5

hypermasculinity, 128–29

"hysteria," 26–27

imperialism, 54, 67, 91

infrastructure, 47, 54, 60–64, 68, 106

Inter-American Court of Human Rights, 33–34, 54, 71, 108, 124

International Caravan for Justice, 10, 13, 32, 63, plate 1

International Day for the Eradication of Violence against Women, 124

International Women's Day, 77

intersectionality, 8–9, 42

intimidation, by state, 75, 120–21, plate 4

intra-activity, 47

Jaguares (musical group), xvii

Jalisco, xxii

Juache Laguna, Idaly, 108n1

"Juárez" (makeup collection), xv

Juárez Women's Institute, 74

Justicia Para Davíd Meza, 31n6

Justicia Para Nuestras Hijas, 22–23, 126

Lear, 62

Lefebvre, Henri, 83, 85, 101

legal categorization, 124–27

Levinas, Emmanuel, 89–91, 93–98

Leyva, Veronica, 50, 52, 54, 57, 59, 132

Lleva, Veronica, 29–30

Lomas de Poleo, 53 fig. 2.1, 61, 61n7, 64, 96–97, 97 fig. 4.4

López, Jennifer, xvii

MAC Cosmetics, xv

MacKinnon, Catharine, xxiii

Maclovio (artist), 45, 80 fig. 3.3, 87–88, 100–104, 109–10

maquiladoras, 8, 14, 47, 49–52, 49n2, 53n3, 110, 132–33

"maqui-loca," 91, 91n3

Marquez, Jessica, 48n1, 51, 56

Marx, Karl, 52, 59, 64

masculinity, 128–29

materialism. See new materialism; vital materialism

materiality: theoretical debates on, 2–9

matter: defined, 107. See also vibrant matter

"matter-memory-makers," 69–70, 74–81, 76 fig. 3.2, 80 fig. 3.3

memory, public, 70–71

menstruation, 60–61

mental hospital, 26

Mesa de Mujeres, 108n1

Mesa de Seguridad, xixn4

methodological approaches, 9–15

Mexico Solidarity Network, 63n8

Meza, Davíd, 31–32, 31n6

Michoacán, xxii

militarization, xix, 37–41, 108

"mnemonicide," 70

Monárrez-Fragozo, Julia, xviii, xxi fig. 0.2, 116

monuments: government, 70–74, 73 fig. 3.1; by Mothers, 71–72, 75–81, 76 fig. 3.2, 80 fig. 3.3, 81–82, 87–88, plate 2–plate 3

Morales, Jessica, xix, 81

Morales, Ramona, 22, 26

Morelos, xxii

Morfín Otero, Guadalupe, xxiii, 35–36

"Mother-activist" groups, xviii; antagonism with government, 21, 23–24; "cotton field" monument and, 71–74, 73 fig. 3.1; emergence of, 22–23; gains by, in Wave Two, 32–33; harassment of, 24–25; as "hysterical," 26–27; monuments by, 71–72, 75–81, 76 fig. 3.2, 80 fig. 3.3, 81–82,

87–88, plate 2–plate 3; tactics to divide, 26; as truth tellers, 29
Mothers' Caravan for Justice, 63n8
movies, xvii
Mujeres de Juárez, Las (Amavizca), xvii
"Mujeres de Juárez, Las" (Tigres del Norte), xvii
Mujeres de Negro, xviii, 20
Mulleavey, Kate, xv
Mulleavey, Laura, xv
Municipal Institute for Women, 129
murals. *See* "Faces of Feminicidio" murals; government murals
Murder City (Bowden), xvii
myth, xvii, 43–44

"narco wars," 8, 10, 37–38, 40–42. *See also* organized crime
National Action Party (PAN), xixn4, 127
National Border Program, 49
necropolitics, 37–38
neoliberalism, 8, 46–47, 50–51, 54–56, 59, 62–63, 67, 91, 109–10, 131–34
new materialism, 1; assemblages in, 46–48, 67–68; intra-activity in, 47; posthumanism and, 5–7; tenets of, 4–5; turn to, 2–4; vibrant matter in, 107–22
norms, gendered: cultural, 127–29; disruption of, 57–59
North American Free Trade Agreement (NAFTA), 12, 14, 48n1, 50–53, 63, 78, 91, 109
novels, xvii
Nuestras Hijas de Regreso a Casa, 55–56

object-oriented affect, 89, 100–103
"organic intellectual," 23
organized crime, 40, 42, 110, 125–26

Paseo del Norte Human Rights Center, 111
patriarchy, 128–29
Pena Garcia, Jessica Leticia, 108n1

"percepticide," 99–100
Pérez Montes, Maria Guadalupe, 108–9, 108n1
Pérez Ortiz, Maria de los Angeles, xx fig. 0.1
Pérez Verdugo, Felix L., 48n1, 57–58, 128, 132–33
Phillips Manufacturing, 60
Pink Nopál, 44
place, 81–85
Plaza de Mayo, 74–75, 89
Portillo, Lourdes, xviii
posthumanism, 1, 3–7, 9, 46, 73, 90, 97, 134
pregnancy, 61, 130
pregnancy tests, 60–61, 67
ProNaf, 49–50
prostitution, 12, 28, 59, 105, 109, plate 6
public memory, 70–71

Radford, Jill, xxii
Ramirez Muñoz, Deysi, 108n1
Ramos Mancha, Lidia, 108n1
Ramos Monárrez, Laura Berenice, 33–34
rape, 55, 62, 125, 128
Rebeldes, Los, 31n5
Red Mesa de Mujeres, 44, 129
remains, search for, 108–22, 108n1, 113 fig. 5.1, 114–17, 115n3, 117 fig. 5.2, plate 11–plate 12. *See also* vibrant matter
resistance, 65–66
Revolutionary Institutional Party (PRI), xixn4, 127
Reyes, Josefina, 41, 41 fig. 1.2
rhetoric: agency and, 69, 134; of government, 41–42, 130; materiality and, 2, 136; misogynistic, 42; of Mothers, 29; new materialism and, 2; in "the field," 11–13
rhetorical constraints, 13–15
rhetorical opportunities, 13–15
Rivas, Letty, 99, 102, 102n5

Rocha, Lluvia, 35, 41–42, 83, 87, 89n1, 90–91, 94–97, 99–101, 129–30
Rodarte, xv
Rodriguez, Susana, 108–9
Rosas Rojas Juárez, 44
Ruiz Zavala, Érika Ivonne, 28–29
Russell, Diana, xxii

sanitation, 65–66, 66n11
Sarmiento, Adriana, 90–91, 92 fig. 4.1
scapegoating, 31–32, 31n5
scholar-activist subject position, 9–11
Señorita Extraviada (film), xviii
Serrano Escobar, Enrique, 43
Sharif, Abdel Latif Sharif, 31n5
shopping-mall directories, 82–83, 84 fig. 3.4
Sisters of Tonatzín, 65–66
sit-in, 53n3
space, 81–85
state. See government
suicide, xixn6, 25
superhighway, 64, 64n10

Tarango Ronquillo, Maria Angelina, 69, 75
Terrazas Ortega, Jessica, 108n1
therapeutic discourse, 26–27
"thing power": agency and, 69; defined, 69; in new materialism, 4–5, 9; place and, 81–85; space and, 81–85
Tigres del Norte, Los (musical group), xvii
"Todos Somos Juárez" campaign, 44
toilets, 65–66, 66n11, 133, plate 5

torture: confession via, 31–32, 31n6; of victims, xvi, xxii, 83n4
tourism, xviii, 49, 82, 82n3
trash cans, 83

unions, 53, 53n3, 63, 65, 66n11, 132
United States: culpability of, 54–56; forced exile to, 37; and National Border Program, 49. See also North American Free Trade Agreement (NAFTA)

Vagina Monologues, The, xvii
Valenzuela, Consuelo, 27
Vargas, Irma, 102
vibrant matter: agency and, 107–8; and Arroyo del Navajo, 108–10; and citizen action committees, 110–11; and enactment of role of state, 112–14; examples of, 107; and searches for remains, 114–15; and struggle for recognition, 116–18
Viesca, Oscar, 112, 114–15
Viesca, Silvia, 112
Villalobos, Juanita, 26
Virgin of Juárez, The (film), xvii
virgin/whore dichotomy, 59
vital materialism, 107–8, 121
Voces sin Echo, xviii, 20, 75

Washington Valdez, Diana, 31n4, 39–40
Wave One, 19–20
Wave Two, 21–36
Wave Three, 37–43

Zavala, Guadalupe, 28–29

NEW DIRECTIONS IN RHETORIC AND MATERIALITY
BARBARA A. BIESECKER, WENDY S. HESFORD, AND CHRISTA TESTON,
SERIES EDITORS

Current conversations about rhetoric signal a new attentiveness to and critical appraisal of material-discursive phenomena. New Directions in Rhetoric and Materiality provides a forum for responding to and extending such conversations. The series publishes monographs that pair rhetorical theory with an analysis of material conditions and the social-symbolic labor circulating therein. Books in the series offer a "new direction" for exploring the everyday, material, lived conditions of human, nonhuman, and extra-human life—advancing theories around rhetoric's relationship to materiality.

Not One More! Feminicidio on the Border
NINA MARIA LOZANO

Visualizing Posthuman Conservation in the Age of the Anthropocene
AMY D. PROPEN

Precarious Rhetorics
EDITED BY WENDY S. HESFORD, ADELA C. LICONA, AND CHRISTA TESTON